HOW TO COUNTER GROUP MANIPULATION TACTICS

HOW TO COUNTER GROUP MANIPULATION TACTICS

THE TECHNIQUES OF UNETHICAL CONSENSUS-BUILDING UNMASKED

by

B. K. Eakman

To Valerie
Best regards,
Beverly Eakman
9-21-13

ISBN: 145051913X
EAN-13: 9781450519137

2011 Edition

For More Information Contact
Midnight Whistler Publishers
http://www.midnightwhistler.com
info@midnightwhistler.com

GETTING CLOBBERED IN MEETINGS?

LEARN HOW TO COUNTER GROUP MANIPULATION TACTICS

Before you volunteer for that curriculum committee, school violence task force or focus group; before you run for school board or PTA president: Find out who the professional manipulators are and how they're going to get you to stick your foot in your mouth.

First, you'll need to recognize:

Provocateurs, agitators, change agents

"Psychologically controlled environments"

The principles of "scientific coercion"

A rigged audience or committee

Techniques used to ostracize people

Phony consensus strategies

International Human Rights Award-Winner, Beverly Eakman, veteran educator, science writer, Washington political speechwriter, and author of the blockbuster education books, *CLONING OF THE AMERICAN MIND: Eradicating Morality Through Education* (Huntington House) and *WALKING TARGETS: How Our Psychologized Classrooms are Producing a Nation of Sitting Ducks,* has given dozens of seminars on Part IV of this critical text: ***"How to Counter Professional Manipulators in Small and Large Groups."***

She has been a guest on over 600 talk shows, with glowing reviews from the National Association of Scholars, the American Association of Physicians & Surgeons, and others.

Here she offers a hands-on workshop in strategies used to silence parents and concerned citizens and generate a predetermined consensus on controversial issues.

"It's time to stop trying to fight wars armed, only with the rules of etiquette" says Eakman.

In this latest, updated version of her seminar, you will learn to:

- ***Think like a direct marketing agent and frame the debate.***
- ***Understand the principles of psych-war.***
- ***Counter the Delphi Technique and the Tavistock Method and other unethical consensus-building strategies.***
- ***Recognize typical manipulative lead-in lines used by the pros.***
- ***Turn the tables on facilitators.***
- ***Catch the pros when they try to re-define terms.***
- ***Create a psychological environment.***
- ***Discover the five basic steps to indoctrination.***
- ***Master the art of argument.***
- ***Inoculate yourself against group-think and "thought disruption."***
- ***Control the "environment of thought."***

PREFACE

A few years ago, when I was working for a federal agency, a combination sexual harassment-AIDS awareness workshop was mandated for employees. We had to select from one of three days.

As most of us expected, it was all about political correctness—which, oddly enough, didn't bother some of my colleagues one way or the other. After all, they figured they were paid to endorse the policies of the current administration, whatever those may be and however much they might conflict with policies of a previous, or future, administration. So, recognizing that this was a "required" workshop, most were anxious to give the impression that they were value-neutral. Thus, my colleagues smiled and preened. The lady who served as workshop moderator began by asking: "What pops into your heads as soon as I say: AIDS, HIV, sexual orientation." We were all supposed to call out something. So, most said what they thought the woman wanted to hear: "homophobia," "fear," "intolerance."

Then she turned out the lights and showed a short film featuring interviews with homosexuals and others—they may have been actors—all of whom, of course, decried "stereotyping" and went on to express incredulity that something so "normal" as same-sex attraction could cause a person to be ostracized.

Afterward, the moderator worked, without much success, to generate discussion, and then turned to the topic of to how one couldn't get AIDS, or the virus that causes it, HIV, from the fellow in the next cubicle, or by using the same restrooms, and so on, which of course, was only minimally accurate as long as one doesn't accidentally take in a bodily fluid, such as splash-ups from drinking faucets, touch a toothpaste tube that had been contaminated with a toothbrush used by an infected person and whatnot.

What neither my colleagues, nor the moderator herself, knew was that there was someone in the room who not only understood we weren't getting the whole picture, but who also was quite familiar with consensus-building, where psychological manipulation is a sucker's game.

After listening to the politically correct spiel for half an hour, I raised my hand: "Excuse me, I have a question," I said.

Now, this was music to the moderator's ears because it meant, she *thought,* that she might be starting to connect with her unwilling subjects, most of whom were looking at their watches. I said:

"I think all of us here know the risk of catching AIDS or HIV from the person in the next office or bathroom stall is minimal. That's not what concerns us. What many of us *are* concerned about is the compromised immune systems of those who indulge in risky sexual behavior, individuals who go on to get strains of pneumonia, tuberculosis and other highly contagious diseases that are very resistant to antibiotics and other treatments. What materials have you brought us that address this issue?"

Well, the lady was flummoxed. She'd never expected the question, had no literature, and no snappy response. So, I yawned and stretched and said: "Well, if there's nothing in your repertoire that addresses real concerns like this, I think we're done here."

I got up and proceeded to walk out, ***whereupon everybody else followed me out of the room***.

This is how you co-opt phony consensus meetings, and get others, including the weaker fence-sitters, to join you.

So, what, exactly, did I do?

Actually, several levels of effort were at work here, even though it all appeared very smooth:

- First, I didn't give the moderator anything to arouse suspicion, either through something I said or my body language, until she unintentionally provided an opening, which I figured she would, eventually. So, she had no means of shutting me out.
- Secondly, I didn't get distracted by her opening gambit to create an "us" mentality with her "we're-all-on-the-same-team" questions. In fact, I turned the tactic back on *her* ("What ***many of us*** are concerned about is....")!
- Third, I never referred directly to myself; I kept saying "many of us" or "we" [are concerned, etc.], thereby making it difficult for her to ostracize me.
- Finally, I affected a calm, lay-back, non-confrontational, even bored demeanor throughout, which drew my colleagues in.

All these tactics are grounded in the axioms and rules of Psych-War. That's what you will be studying and practicing in this course.

GENERAL INTRODUCTION

How many times have you had the unsettling experience of being treated as a troublemaker as soon as you question or raise an objection to a school policy, a textbook, a course of study, a new county regulation, or a community proposal?

You may have noticed that questioning today is tantamount to being "uncooperative"—a big no-no. Baby Boomers may remember when questioning authority and even thumbing one's nose at the teacher was deemed a noble act, back when Marxism in America was young, in the 1960s and 70s. Predictably, that attitude morphed into something quite different. Once grown, Boomers found they "didn't get no respect" and weren't taken seriously unless they came off as authoritative—i.e., advanced degrees, connections, and status with a credible organization.

Many hippie-Boomers reversed course and became the very beings they once despised: authoritarian and dogmatic little fascists whose goal in life was tell others how to live and think. They became PR agents of sorts, specializing in market research, data-gathering, promotional advertising and political strategy. What they didn't know back in college was that the Marxists who infiltrated our country, organized protests and initiated a campaign of "civil disobedience" had targeted their age group via the universities and government bureaucracies in those same years. These "agents of change" were trained provocateurs—the best there was. America's Boomer population learned from them and handed down the techniques to their own progeny—sometimes knowingly, sometimes not.

Today, be it the workplace, a community forum, airport security, or the PTA, *team spirit* (the old Marxists called it "collective spirit") is valued above individual conscience and over unique ideas. Nobody is supposed to cry "foul" or "rock the boat." The validity of your complaint or concern is of little account if it flies in the face of team spirit. For that reason, it's not unusual for citizens today to leave meetings, focus groups and task forces frustrated and angry, suspecting deep down that there was a better way to have made their point or shut down the steamroller effect that inevitably ends in resisters signing on to whatever the group leader wanted in the first place. Sometimes earnest individuals even wind up in a confrontation when all they meant to do was inject a different viewpoint. Schoolchildren, as we shall see, can encounter similar problems in the classroom. It's all Marxist tactics, just dressed differently.

Unfortunately, most laypersons—and sometimes even legislators—don't realize they're dealing with well-trained provocateurs the minute they set foot in the room with chairpersons serving as "moderators" of a discussion. Often they are professional manipulators—variously referred to as provocateurs, agitators, change agents and even facilitators or moderators, the latter two being better disguised than the rest.

By whichever term they go by, however, these people are typically professionals brought in from outside the community, the school district or whatever is forum of choice for a meeting. They are paid by a special interest—usually second and third parties so as to mask the real money trail—such as the National Education Association's Uniserve and National Training Laboratory; one of billionaire George Soros' "philanthropic" arms; or the Education Commission of the States (the latter launched by the Carnegie Foundation for the Advancement of Teaching, but popularly believed to be a government, or "state," agency). The professional manipulators are there to "sell" you on an idea, program or initiative you probably would not approve of if presented on its own merits. And there's the rub.

To have your view heard and taken seriously, you must know, first, how to recognize psychological manipulation and either work around it or shut it down. You must be able to reframe the debate, take it *away* from your adversary, and argue the issue on ***your*** terms, not on your opponent's. To do this requires mastering certain principles of argument, then applying them in a group setting, ***under pressure***.

For reasons you'll understand shortly, *it's easier to control a group than it is to control a single individual*. Now, that may seem strange, but it's actually the reason behind attempts to "collectivize" people in a meeting. Professional manipulators, like the amiable "facilitator" with an ulterior motive, will try to maneuver you into a group setting ("we're all in this together, right?"). And that's your first giveaway as to whom you are dealing with—a change agent/agitator or, as I'll be using the term, a *provocateur*. The difference is minor. A group can unwittingly help the provocateur pull the rug from under all potential adversaries—by isolating them, ridiculing them, ostracizing them, and finally overwhelming them.

Attorneys, media commentators, and journalists are among the few who get the training provided in this manual. Most people believe that the best way to get through to an adversary is via a heart-to-heart, fact-based discussion.

That's true only if people are ***honestly*** debating an issue as equals. It's ***not true*** if the debate is ***dis***honest. If a provocateur can generate a mob mentality, and get it to work for him, *control of the agenda* is usually assured.

Thus, Rule Number One: *Never let the other fellow control the debate, or agenda.*

And, by the way, that's how your kids get caught up in all sorts of nastiness—from falling for trashy pop artists, to competing to look like hookers and pimps in school. Teachers and ad agencies both function as "agents of change." So, they ***heighten*** peer pressure (that's "social pressure" to adults) until it functions as ***mob mentality***.

Once that occurs, ideas can be planted that go against 2000 years of civilization. Both children and adults will accept them for no other reason than that the group finds them fashionable. Of course, children are typically undiscerning and have no experience with hard-core manipulation tactics.

But adults are in trouble, too.

Over some 40 years, parents have been convinced by "experts" that both *authoritarianism* and *individualism* are negative, which makes for considerable confusion. The brand of authoritarianism practiced by moderators like the one chairing the federal workshop on sexual harassment and AIDS, the one I walked out on, is considered "above" questioning. We have been conditioned to see these moderators as "experts," and therefore, our "betters." But they are rarely experts in any legitimate field. They are experts in manipulation. Thus, most average folks are ill-equipped to stand up for their principles, much less teach their kids to do so. We fear being censured and insulted. When we feel cornered, we sound hysterical, raise our voices—and assure our doom. That means the provocateur, agitator, change agent, or whatever you wish to call a professional manipulator, gets the *group* to do the dirty work, by "turning" against, or backstabbing, their colleagues. If you ever participated in one of those hippie-era encounter sessions, you will recognize the strategy immediately. It means basically bullying your friends, or anybody else who dares to think for him (or her) self, into adopting the beliefs and ideas of the group.

And we wonder why we have a bullying epidemic in our schools? When adults themselves have been browbeaten for years into adopting a mob mentality, what can we expect from children? You get bullying on steroids!

The mob mentality is achieved by creating what's known in the vernacular of manipulators as a "*psychologically controlled environment*." You will want to disrupt, or better yet, ***pre-empt*** the establishment of a psychologically controlled environment. You will need to understand the strategies and techniques that a provocateur uses to assure the outcome he or she wants, so that you can counter those techniques as you go, *and get others in the group to help you, whether they understand what you are doing or not*. In other words, you have to beat the manipulator at his (or her) own game.

So, be aware, first that:

- **It's easier to control a group than a single individual**.
- **Your opponent should never be allowed to control the debate, or agenda.**
- **It is the beginning of the end if you fall victim to what is known to expert manipulators as a "psychologically controlled environment**."

Many of the principles you will study in this course are take-offs on an ancient Chinese text, *The Art of War*, thought to have been written around 476 BC. This little book has received renewed attention recently, but too few really understand the axioms. For example:

- **A resistance movement is not run according to rules of etiquette.**
- **Those skilled in war subdue the enemy without physical battle.**
- **Deception and surprise are two key principles of battle.**
- **Confuse the enemy's leaders—"if possible, drive them insane."**

From just these four axioms, you can see that *demoralization of the enemy* was a high priority, even back then. Your opponents want to demoralize you; that's the point of all psychological agitation and provocation.

So just who are your real antagonists?

Basically, your enemies are a relatively small, radical cadre of professionals who have been trained to overwhelm a larger body of people, usually for-hire. Sometimes it takes only one person, the guy or gal you thought was chairing your meeting, to engineer a consensus nobody wants. A *facilitator*, for example, is supposed to keep the meeting on track and moving along. But a professional manipulator's entire mission is usually part of a larger offensive to keep the meeting on message, not on track, to promote an agenda nobody expected, and to identify and isolate holdouts, especially when the topic centers on standards of morality, limited government and low taxes.

Sometimes, the giveaway will be what, at first blush, *appears* to be one or more out-of-place persons in your midst—individuals who not only *don't* agree with most of the rest of your group, but who somehow manage to intimidate everyone else. They can blindside a focus group, meeting or committee.

For example, you might attend a meeting concerning same-sex marriage or gay priests in a large church where the membership is very traditional. And here is this individual, or group of individuals nobody recognizes advocating for same-sex marriage and homosexual priests. How come nobody says: "Why do these loudmouths go to church *here*, with a minister and parishioners they couldn't possibly like?"

Instead, "nice" parishioners allow these provocateurs to go on and on, in the spirit of honest debate. In other words, you're more afraid of appearing cantankerous, narrow-minded and inflexible—all politically *in*correct characterizations—than you are of one or more outsiders taking over your meeting and steering it in an entirely different direction. Why is that?

Because you've been conditioned since schooldays that it's proper and right. So you play by the rules, while your adversaries have a blast at your expense.

So, one hint that you may be dealing with professional manipulators is that certain folks sitting in your midst don't seem to fit. Of course, sometimes it's the moderator, or facilitator, who doesn't fit and takes the lead. You may even find that the outspoken oddballs in your group and the moderator are actually in cahoots, that the seemingly random outbursts are choreographed. A consensus will be generated from such a forum and taken by the phony facilitator to your legislators or school officials or other decision-makers and presented as "what the community really wants." Or as a consensus that "everyone" supposedly arrived at.

The dictionary definition of *consensus* is: group solidarity in sentiment and belief and/or general agreement: Unanimity, on the other hand, is defined as: collective opinion. Increasingly, people are hearing the term "consensus," when what our opponents want, in reality, is unanimity, or uniform thinking.

All consensus-building is based on a principle first articulated by the German philosopher Georg Wilhelm Hegel around 1800. He discovered that you can take one firm point of view, and then its opposite, combine them, and come up with a brand new viewpoint—a *synthesis* of the two. This new viewpoint will be the one that all parties are either urged to accept, or tricked into accepting.

So, **a consensus is essentially a collective opinion** that doesn't reflect anyone's opinion. When the collective good is viewed as superior to, ***and more important than***, the individual good (the socialist-globalist view), then *consensus no longer falls into the category of compromise*. *Consensus* is a stronger term, because *the pro and con viewpoints, in a collectivist mindset, no longer exist.* The rightness or wrongness of the original viewpoints is not at issue. *The point is to produce a new ideal, opinion, or value that will be universally supported*—or at least appear to be supported by everyone. And that is the rub —"appears to be."]

The purpose of the various consensus strategies is to ***preserve the illusion that there is lay, or community, participation in policy-related decision-making, when in fact there isn't***. That means something far different from "working out a compromise." When a professional provocateur is, say, trying to get a community behind a unit supporting global warming in your child's high school science curriculum, they know they have to at least pretend to involve parents in the decision and have something to that effect *in writing* when people complain to their legislators in Congress later.

Controlling the "psychological environment"—something I derogatorily call "climate control"—makes it easier for one side to frame the debate and keep you from doing so. A psychologically controlled environment provides a platform from which to operate and prevents individuals from injecting an alternate viewpoint, much less taking back the discussion.

This sets up a kind of *mass neurosis*, because people like you are sitting there are scratching their heads. They know the consensus isn't true. Yet, lie after lie is presented by "reputable" sources that are believed. This leads to a psychological condition known as "cognitive dissonance," meaning that an irreconcilable conflict has been set up. As people become increasingly uncomfortable, they vacillate, lose their frame of reference and become alienated. *Once marginalized, people look for comfort inside the group instead of thinking for themselves.*

Alienated committee members, particularly if they are the backbone of a community, help the provocateur because they get the primary resistance out of the way. ***Alienated people start needing each other more than they need their principles.***

Take a complex subject which carries a requirement for some background in science: **Sustainable Development** and its sister topic, **Sustainable Communities**. You may have heard of these, the latter often repeated under the umbrella term "planned communities," which is not quite the same thing but nevertheless is useful to advocates of **Sustainable Development.**

The definition of **Sustainable Development** is rarely cited by advocates, and for good reason, because the term itself functions as a positive-sounding slogan. The words "sustained" and "developed" carry positive connotations which, of course, make the slogan saleable.

In a remarkably accurate—and telling—description, the popular online encyclopedia, Wikipedia, defines **Sustainable Development** (**SD**) as "a pattern of resource use that aims to meet human needs while preserving the environment so that these needs can be met not only in the present, but also for generations to come." It explains the term as having been coined by the Brundtland Commission to describe development which "meets the needs of the present without compromising the ability of future generations to meet their own needs." If you click on the hyperlink, you discover that the Brundtland Commission is formally known as the **World Commission on Environment and Development** (WCED), a United Nations construct. **SD**, explains Wikipedia, weaves together concerns for the so-called "carrying capacity of natural systems" with "the ***social challenges*** facing humanity." And that should be your first clue that something is "off." This is not a United States idea, it is a United Nations idea, and we already know that the goals of the U.S. and the U.N. are frequently at odds. The U.N. advocates for socialism and the U.S., at least up to the present time, has advocated for self-determination, the opposite of a Nanny State.

In the 1970s "sustainability" was first used to describe an ***economy*** "in equilibrium with basic ecological support systems." Ecologists pointed to a proposals calling for ***Limits to Growth,*** which, again, should have been a telling phrase that set off alarm bells in the U.S. But it didn't, largely due to the naïveté of young adults of the day (like Al Gore, a wealthy, just-out-of-college Ivy League graduate with mediocre grades), who were then being alternately inflamed against "the Establishment" and groomed for "social change" by professional manipulators trained either in, or through, Soviet bloc countries. The mainstream media, by then, was already infiltrated and flush with a new breed of journalist that preferred easy tabloid-type scandals to actually digging deeply for information. To preserve their credentials and status, they were careful to reflect only anti-traditional attitudes.

That left the early environmentalists of the 70's free to create what they called a "steady state economy" in the process of addressing what were often baseless environmental concerns.

SD was soon broken down into three inter-related parts, at least conceptually: environmental sustainability, economic sustainability and sociopolitical sustainability—which means there was more to SD than met the eye. If the whole cloth encompassed economic, environmental and all social/political activity, then such a sweeping agenda obviously would produce a wrenching transformation in *any* society. But it was a particularly lethal mix in a uniquely free United States.

We will address SD in more detail later, but the point here is that anyone who tries to nail down definitions or explain the implications of SD in a group setting is going to be isolated at the get-go. How? If the person can't condense his remarks into a single, oversimplified, slogan-like sentence and tries instead to inform the group as to how the inter-relationships of three SD components produce global governance and compromise national sovereignty, he will be told, politely, that his comments are too long and that, further, the remarks themselves smack of the ramblings of a conspiracy theorist. Chastened by the facilitator as a probable nut-case, this fellow who dares offer some insight into SD will find that the group has moved to save itself by having nothing to do with him. (See Appendices for more on SD and U.N. encroachment into U.S. laws and policies.)

Karl Marx had a theory on the step-by-step process of marginalization, alienation, ostracism and (eventually) total isolation: that people will do almost anything to avoid ridicule and will stay quiet. He was right, and Saul Alinsky (1909-1972), under the banner of a "community organizer," was among the first to use the idea successfully in America. He knew, as did Marxist colleagues like Herbert Marcuse (and later, Bill Ayers), that in a country like ours, which promotes "being popular" from the earliest years—that is, status-seeking and team spirit over independent thought—alienation would be particularly effective. Alinsky started his campaign at the height of the Cold War and Marxist infiltration, in the 1950s, by inciting clueless African-Americans in Chicago and other cities in four states.

Then, like Herbert Marcuse, he moved on to provoking college students on campuses in the 1960s, organizing protests and demonstrations on their parents' tuition money.

In his classic 1971 strategy manual, *Rules for Radicals*, intended for use in America and eventually throughout the free world, Saul Alinsky advises organizers to deliberately antagonize opponents. "The real action is in the enemy's reaction," he wrote. "The enemy properly goaded and guided in his reaction will be your major strength."

The year 1971 was useful in that the Vietnam War had been badly mishandled and could be used to generate violent hostilities among college-age potential draftees under the false banner of "peace and love." University faculties and administration already had been largely penetrated by the left, as were entry-level positions within government itself. So, with the anti-war movement in full swing, and young Boomer collegiates anxious to leave the nest, be their own person and appear mature, the professional "organizers" could be relatively assured their quarry would not understand that they were being played. Organizers such as Alinsky and Marcuse basically "stroked" their victims' egos to make them believe they were far more "aware" than they really were. Unfortunately, they had no experience with the tools of deception, so they were easy marks, flush with overconfidence and idealism. The organizers used that to win over these brash, 17-25 year-olds. That accomplished, they then got down to their real work.

Rule No. 4 in Alinsky's, Rules for Radicals, says: "Make the enemy live up to their own book of rules. You can kill them with this, for they can no more obey their own rules than the Christian church can live up to Christianity."

Saul Alinsky continues by explaining that the "fourth rule carries within it a fifth rule: Ridicule is man's most potent weapon. It is almost impossible to counterattack ridicule. Also, it infuriates the opposition, who then react to your advantage."

As columnist Robert Knight so aptly put it,[1] this strategy means that someone, in effect, can punch you in the stomach and then accuse you of overreacting. A manipulator will take great glee in making fun of everything you hold sacred, then accuse you of being over-sensitive when you balk. He or she will make a mockery of "virtue," ensuring that you and other like-minded people will come off as hypocrites in the media.

A modern-day example would be the 2010 video showing ants crawling across a crucified Christ. Then, in an about-face, the same purveyors of this "artistic" video will howl about censorship the moment Christians object to the use of their tax dollars to promote immorality or an Islamic "Cultural Center" and mosque at Ground Zero in New York City.

This rule also allows socialists in America to quote the Constitution selectively, to take pieces out of context and replicate certain other phrases creating a new, socialist twist. Many examples of this can be found in United Nations' covenants, declarations, proclamations and protocols. If you don't read too closely, these declarations and so forth will seem more or less consistent with the phraseology of Thomas Jefferson, John Adams, James Monroe and Benjamin Franklin

1 "The radical art of deliberate offense," by Robert Knight, *The Washington Times*, Dec. 1, 2010 and "Supernatural hand in Christmas atheism," by Robert Knight, *The Washington Times*, Dec. 24, 2010.

when, in fact, the intent is to bring into question what were actually very clear meanings contained in the U.S. Constitution, the Bill of Rights and the Declaration of Independence. In the U.N.'s Universal Declaration of Human Rights, for example, Thomas Jefferson's line about the "pursuit of happiness" is changed slightly to affirm that "all peoples have a right to leisure," to holidays and to reasonable work hours. This sounds lovely, of course, but it differs from the individual right to "pursue happiness." Reading on, one finds that the U.N. is advocating for a State that *guarantees* happiness.

Another take on this little game of ridicule and ostracism is for the provocateur to whip dissenters into a teeth-clenching, frenzy of anger, until they become so <u>out</u>raged, <u>en</u>raged, and frustrated, that they start lashing out in all directions—unfocused and in disarray. Such individuals will not be good spokespersons for their cause in the media but, rather, will come off as hysterical. Many of the student protesters of the 1960s who thought themselves so mature actually sounded like addled-brained drug-addicts even when they were not because of their frenzied demeanor. Their demonstrations of righteous anger only worked because the media made it appear that crowds were bigger than they actually were, covered them continually, and because chaos and anarchy was part of the "promotional package." Chaos and anarchy—kids behaving badly—could be used later to initiate draconian surveillance mechanisms like "traffic" cameras, roving wiretaps and searches and seizures without probable cause, all in the name of "safety." By then, folks would "buy into," or at least succumb to, a vast increase in regimentation, surveillance and over-regulation.

So, understand that *professional provocateurs are not interested in any exchange of ideas.* They aren't writing well-considered philosophical discourses to each other like the Founding Fathers did. They want to "drive the opposition insane"—in other words, cause you to act irrationally.

The hypocritical way in which rules are applied to those with politically incorrect views, like the little boy in Rhode Island, who was sent home for wearing a patriotic hat with tiny toy soldiers attached (a terrorist act), while youngsters with their pants hanging off their backsides are deemed to have a "right" to their individuality: This is *provocation*—all calculated to "drive us crazy," as Sun Tzu would have put it, or as Saul Alinsky would say, to "infuriate the opposition, who then [must] react...." This is the stuff of Marx's Theory of Alienation. The only shades of difference lie in some of the newer, more creative methods of application.

As the frustration level is turned up, eventually someone somewhere will go off the deep end. A bomb explodes at an abortion clinic. A "survivalist" holes up in a secluded area and starts shooting "trespassers." This thrills our adversaries no end, because then they can claim that *all* people who oppose abortion, and *all* people who want to be left alone are "dangerous."

Which brings us back to the beginning: we're afraid to object. No wonder we're getting clobbered!

Now remember, this is a crash course. Professional agitators and provocateurs spend weeks, months, even years perfecting the techniques I'm going to show you. Throwing hardball tactics back in the face of a professional provocateur is risky unless you have practiced, practiced, practiced. You may memorize how to do it, theoretically, but without practice you are likely to modify the techniques just enough to botch them under stress: Too much (or too little) emphasis on certain words, a telling facial expression: these can give away your hand, which you don't want to do.

So, you will need to understand rationales and strategies, memorize the various Psych-War principles, then get with somebody and practice the actual techniques, which are presented here in the form of scenarios that have actually occurred somewhere in the United States. Then, take the Self-Test in the back. If you require advanced instruction—for example, if you are running for public office or facing Senate confirmation hearings—go on to the Advanced Course, then take the Final Exam in the back of the manual.

With all this in mind, here is an outline version of the topics covered in this course:

- **Learning to recognize a "psychologically controlled environment."**
- **Identifying the professional agitator/provocateur.**
- **Examining the components of psych-war, including:**
    - **"scientific coercion"**
    - **controlled-stress situations**
    - **opinion management**
- **Studying the weaknesses of the liberal-leftist, one-world-government mindset.**

- **Learning to undercut faulty, distorted and biased arguments of opponents that you will encounter in meetings, committees and focus groups, including:**
    - **types of reasoning**
    - **typical fallacies**
    - **exposing fallacies in a group setting**
- **Understanding the difference between single-issue propaganda vs. large-scale lobbying, public relations, advertising, "educational" or "awareness" campaigns, and attack strategies.**
- **Recognizing tools used by a provocateur to diffuse or deflect criticism, such as:**
    - **kingpins of the Illiteracy Cartel**
    - **the "snoop survey"**
    - **the "attack manual"**
- **Squelching the techniques used to rebuff citizens and parents who complain or balk, including:**
    - **the infamous 7-point working strategy to rebuff complainants**
    - **how opponents craft testimony to mislead participants in hearings and other formal discussions**
    - **subtle methods of applying censorship and litmus tests**
    - **"negative" and "extreme" stereotyping and labels**

You will also learn how to:

- **Neutralize consensus-building techniques, such as:**
    - **slogans**
    - **redefined terms**
    - **deflections**
    - **alienation and isolation tactics**
    - **labels, stereotypes, and implied smears**
- **Garner the help of other group members without giving away your role to the agitator or facilitator.**
- **Force the provocateur/facilitator to reveal his/her real agenda without showing yours first.**
- **Discern the difference between a debate, a discussion, and a hostile setting.**
- **Teach your child to recognize indoctrination techniques:**
    - **the five phases of indoctrination**
    - **what information is "private"**
    - **how to handle a psychometric exercise**
    - **how to avoid group-think**
    - **encounter-style activities**
    - **the relationship between group-think and peer (or social) pressure;**
    - **how social pressure can be used as a tool to ostracize independent thinkers; and**
    - **school activities that your kids should report to *you*.**

BEGINNER & INTERMEDIATE COURSE

Section 1.- "CLIMATE" CONTROL

One problem is that most of us don't think like direct marketing agents. Our adversaries do. We care about integrity—i.e., the end doesn't always justify the means. The opposition doesn't. We worry that others might get hurt if we speak out. The Education Establishment doesn't give one hoot who gets hurt in the process. Whether it's magazines, billboards, brochures, newspaper columns, speeches, press conferences, or grant proposals, psychological impact is considered paramount to your opponents—not the facts, not anybody's precious principles, and certainly not right or wrong.

If you have read my book, *CLONING OF THE AMERICAN MIND,* you're somewhat familiar with rigged consensus-building. But for those who aren't, a little background is in order.

Consensus-Building – As indicated in the Introduction, the strict definition of consensus is group solidarity in sentiment and belief and/or general agreement. Unanimity, on the other hand, is defined as collective opinion. Increasingly, people are hearing the term "consensus," when what our opponents want, in reality, is unanimity, or uniform thinking.

Consensus-building comes from the old Hegelian view that you can manipulate policy by "public demand" if you maneuver unsuspecting citizens into taking the predominating opinion and combine it with its opposite, thereby coming up with a brand new standpoint that supposedly reflects one that all parties can accept. This, then, passes for compromise, and the compromise is taken to legislators by the professional manipulator and presented as what the community, the PTA, church membership or other public group wants.

But *consensus* does not mean *compromise*. A **consensus is essentially a collective opinion** that isn't necessarily reflective of anybody's private view. Manipulators get away with this because the collective good (or "team") trumps the individual—a socialist concept.

The purpose of the various consensus strategies is to preserve the illusion that there is lay, or community, *participation* in policy-related decision-making that will restrict your movements, abridge your individual rights, raise your taxes and generally make your life more complicated. So, obviously, free and open discussion or debate is not in the interests of today's policymakers, or their hirelings (that is, the provocateurs sent to chair their meetings).

The pretense of public participation is preserved. It looks like a duck and walks like a duck to the untrained eye, but it isn't a duck—it's deception at its finest.

The Delphi Technique is just one unethical method of achieving a deceptive consensus on controversial topics. A well-trained provocateur, usually posing as a facilitator, will deliberately pit one faction against another to make the favored side appear "sensible" and any opposing view ridiculous.

The setting or type of group in which the technique is used is immaterial. The logic behind its success is that most groups tend to share a particular knowledge base and display a certain set of identifiable characteristics. The provocateur wants to locate those smaller factions within the larger group.

Provocateurs, or agitators, often call themselves "facilitators" because that sounds neutral. But what these pros really do is to work the group over to ensure a predetermined outcome, which they call a "consensus." If the discussion is "facilitated" properly, all participants will emerge believing that the decision reached was their own idea. Only later will some realize they were duped.

Donning his or her facilitator hat, the provocateur encourages each person in a group to express concerns about the program, project, or policy in question. S/he listens attentively, elicits input, forms "task forces," urges participants to make lists, and in going through these motions, s/he disrupts everybody's train of thought and learns something about each group member. As an agitator, s/he is trained to identify the leaders, the "loud mouths," the weak and non-committal members, who may change sides during an argument.

The provocateur first will try to become an accepted member of the larger group, but later will turn factions of the group against its own members.

Suddenly, the amiable facilitator will become "devil's advocate." Using the "divide and conquer" principle, s/he pits one faction against the other, making those whose views that are not desired appear ridiculous, unknowledgeable, inarticulate, or dogmatic. S/he deftly augments tension, exacerbates disagreements. If the stage was set properly during the list-building phase, a well-trained provocateur will be able to predict the reactions of most members of a group. Individuals opposing a desired policy or program will find themselves shut out.

The Delphi Technique works. It is effective with parents, teachers, school children, and community groups. The "targets" rarely, if ever, realize that they are being manipulated. If they do suspect what is happening, they usually figure it out about two hours late—after they signed on to an initiative they didn't want.

Suppose a desired policy like support for hybrid vehicles is placed on the table. The provocateur utilizes a "selective hearing" process so that only those questions that support the predetermined policy—such as, say, tax incentives for purchasing electric-gas combination automobiles—is placed on the table for discussion. The only opposing arguments permitted will be those the provocateur deems helpful in escalating tensions later. So, if you point out that plugging a car into an electrical outlet to charge it up uses fossil fuels in the process of generating the electricity, and you know this is not going to be the "preferred" view, don't be taken in when the facilitator acknowledges your suggestion. Remain on guard.

The provocateur, acting as a moderator, guides the discussion so that it doesn't get away from him/her. This means that this facilitator-operative frames the debate and is careful not to let go. Before you know it, some participants will begin to adopt a phase-in approach to mandatory purchase of hybrid autos, complete with penalties down the road for refusing, as if it were their own idea, *and they will be manipulated into pressuring any holdouts into accepting the proposition*.

Why Delphi Works

Consensus strategies like Delphi utilize Karl Marx's Theory of Alienation, alluded to earlier, which states that folks will do just about anything to avoid losing face. What happens is that manipulators have learned that there's a switch that confuses and freezes normal responses. Aware that something is going wrong, and unable to explain, define, or confront it, people find themselves tongue-tied.

Linguistics professor Dean Gotcher, Director of the Institute of Authority Research, explains that there appears to be a trigger mechanism that cuts off one's awareness of impending danger and suppresses the ability to resist, resulting in indecision, and eventually capitulation.

Between the computer and word of mouth, it is fairly easy to pre-select individuals who are most likely to agree or disagree with a proposal and "pack" an audience. Participants against a facilitator-desired proposal are frequently included, too, but they are screened to ensure that they will not be particularly articulate, or that their voice will come off as shrill and hysterical, or that they already have a reputation for being unorganized. So don't be overly flattered if you are *asked* to serve on a committee or task force.

Resisting Delphi

The key to resistance, especially in highly charged, well-organized situations, lies in controlling the environment of thought.

An environment of thought means determining what a group of individuals is going to think about, and for how long. For example, the major media outlets decided that Michael Jackson's death was a hot topic; so hot, in fact, that it could be made to divert attention from more important news. Remember, whoever controls the debate, or agenda, controls the substance of what is going on, be it a discussion, political issues to be addressed (as in a campaign), what news is aired and what gets "spiked," even the kinds of music going out over the airwaves. If such control is achieved by an experienced manipulator in a group setting (i.e., a meeting, focus group, committee, task force, etc.), no questions will be explored and no views will be publicized that deviate from the pre-decided topics.

Another tool in the arsenal of pros is the ability to make "facts" and "truths" interchangeable. What's the difference between a *fact* and a truth?

Making truths and facts interchangeable involves easing individuals away from thoughts concerning how they personally feel on a topic, in the context of their own experience. This is accomplished by placing members of the group into a hypothetical environment that is essentially foreign to their experience, but which requires their involvement—that is, placing members of the group into a what-would-you-do-if situation. And, by the way, this is why school tests and questionnaires also use the technique of posing hypothetical, what-would-you-do-if questions—to place students in an environment that is foreign to their experience but which requires their involvement to "pass" the test. Done correctly, each individual in the group—or in the case of a pupil questionnaire, each child—will move from traditional (or "fixed") beliefs to a transitional mode of thought in which facts become murky, and "truth" or "principles" are in conflict. From there, the various views people hold can be reworded by the "facilitator" or teacher for the "benefit" of the group, until the opinions you walked in the door with become watered down, distorted, or ill-defined. (We will experiment later with the "hypothetical environment.")

So, the "facilitator" is basically there to sell you something you don't want or need—a program, a curriculum, an activity, viewpoint, or a process. They are not there to help the city council, community, PTA, or any other group decide what to do. They are there to get you to do what they, or (more likely) their employers, want you to do. To accomplish that, the professional will attempt to trick everyone into believing that the program, curriculum, activity, or process was their own idea. From there, your group will be manipulated, so that those who are still subconsciously saying, "Wait a minute, this isn't my idea," are either convinced to change sides or are overwhelmed by the larger group.

Your job is to force the facilitator to expose his or her agenda as early on as possible, before the facilitator or anyone else gets you to define yours.

Shutting Down Delphi

So, what do you have to do *first* to counteract someone else's psychological environment? [Think before continuing.]

Answer: First, determine what the real issue is. You may, for example, find advertised, ahead of time, some theme for a meeting which later turns out to be quite different. Once you get there, everyone will be encouraged to make lists and talk. The goal is to "feel out the group"; get a handle on where everyone is coming from. So the thing to do is stay quiet for awhile. Don't give the provocateur anything to work with until you know why you're really there.

After you have determined the issue and committed to keeping quiet, ask yourself: What is my basic position on this issue. Remember it.

That sounds easy, but with all the noise and discussion, it is easy to be drawn off-topic. Other people, of course, will have the opposite view. Remember, what the provocateur wants is a synthesis of two opposing positions, which will be called a compromise, but it won't be. It will be whatever position the provocateur's boss wants it to be!

For example, suppose there is a meeting of the Camden, New Jersey, City Council. Camden is a dangerous, crime-ridden town which, like so many other major cities, is also facing more than a $25 million budget deficit. Because of Camden's reputation for crime, the tax base is dwindling. Middle-class families are moving away, leaving more lower-class wage earners. How is the city going to extract more money through taxes to get the budget deficit down in this situation?

Obviously, one way is through cutbacks. Another is through hidden taxes. Some members of the Council might decide they need to drum up support via an open, public meeting. They hire a professional facilitator (manipulator) to chair the meeting, with the understanding that the citizens of Camden must be led to believe it is in their interest to raise taxes. The manipulator comes up with a plan, an agenda. If you cut back the one thing that people really need, then they will approve a hike in their taxes. In a high-crime area, what is the one thing residents and shopkeepers need? Police. Cut back the police force and pretty soon you'll get public support behind a tax increase.

So, how will the provocateur spin this meeting? Will it be called "a meeting about cutting back law enforcement"?

Answer: Probably not. It's going to be called a meeting about the *deficit crisis*. The word "crisis" will get people's attention. And certainly a $25 million debt is a crisis.

What is the first thing that average citizens intending to weigh in at this meeting need to do?

Answer: Determine the issue. The issue is really "spending priorities," not the city's deficit crisis and certainly not law enforcement. Not for this meeting. So, you will have to keep thinking the term "spending priorities" over and over while the facilitator is off on various tangents about cutbacks and crises.

Let's take another example: a proposal to get a sex education program implemented into the first grade.

What is the first thing you do?

Answer: Again, determine the issue.

Will the issue, the group's reason for meeting, be presented as a proposal to implement sex education for first-graders?

Answer: Probably not. The issue will be presented as the problem of AIDS, teen pregnancy, or youngsters' sexual activity. This is what is meant by the use of deception. Nobody has to actually lie. All they have to do is withhold the truth—and allow you to draw mistaken assumptions.

So, what is the real issue, then? The real issues are the appropriateness of the curriculum and who teaches it.

Before you go to the meeting, find out who the presenters are going to be. Who are the vested interests; that is, who stands to benefit financially from this meeting? This will tell you a whole lot about whether there may be some program to sell to the district.

Now, the district might come up with an abstinence program, so you don't want to jump to conclusions. But even if that is on the table, you can be relatively sure the audience will be packed (with Planned Parenthood people, for example) to ensure abstinence is never adopted. So your problem will remain the same: To determine the real issue, and decide your position on it.

Now, suppose your position is: "Sexual activity outside of marriage is wrong." What's the antithesis, the opposite, of this position?

Answer: "Sexual activity outside of marriage is acceptable." Or, as it will likely be presented: "Kids will do it anyway whether you approve or not."

Now, toward what synthesis will the "facilitator" likely try to move the group or community—before any mention of a new program to be launched at your school? [*Think before continuing.*]

Answer: The desired compromise position will probably go something like this: "Inasmuch as teen sexual activity is unavoidable, youngsters who indulge must do so safely, without consequences, and without hurting anybody else."

Once the provocateur can get everyone to agree to this position, then s/he can go about garnering support for anything from AIDS posters for kindergartners to condoms for second-graders. Anyone who balks will be reminded about the group consensus until most people "behave themselves." Some will actually believe the consensus makes sense. Nobody will want to appear stuffy to the group, even though most members may have held the same thesis you did when they walked in.

Notice that the counterculture never compromises. This is one of the tell-tale giveaways that you're dealing with a "pro." For example, if the topic is the environment, you will never hear a word about global warming being just one theory. If the topic is vouchers or tuition tax credits, you will never hear a word from the "facilitator" about working together with home-schoolers. Consensus, in the context we're discussing it, is always a one-way street. Traditionalists will do all the "compromising"—meaning you'll be railroaded into giving in.

The key to the facilitator's success, then, is controlling the environment of thought, holding on to the reins of the discussion. Your task is not to let that happen. Not at the beginning. Not an hour later. Not ever.

Section 2. - WHAT IS PSYCHOLOGICAL MANIPULATION?

The right combination of marketing and agitation results in the ability to manipulate people psychologically. Done properly, one *can* fool most of the people most of the time. Psychological manipulation relies on four key maneuvers:

a. Redefining
b. Redirecting
c. Consensus-building
d. Marketing

The aim is to legitimize, then institutionalize, unpopular and bogus policies before people know what has hit them. The resulting marketing package is *not* a one-size-fits-all; rather, different packages are targeted to different elements of society—the business community, the intelligentsia, religious leaders, lawmakers, etc.

Take redefining terms: The public misinterprets the terms modifying behavior targeting attitudes, and outcomes. Most of the public assumes that behavior means "conduct," that attitude means "temperament," and that outcomes mean "standards." Not so. In the jargon of psychology, modifying behavior means "altering beliefs," attitude means "viewpoint," and outcomes are the world views a child is supposed to leave school with.

A person's attitudes, taken together, comprise his belief system. People typically are unaware of their belief system, as it is made up of unconscious, automatic assumptions and responses to life situations.

So, the first step in engineering a widespread change of viewpoint is to redefine the terms, and to ensure that the new terminology "feels good."

Slogans help to redefine terms. Appealing marketing slogans like "Smart Growth," "critical thinking," and "urban sprawl" are coined by ad agencies (which, in turn, are paid for by well-funded advocates) to promote and disseminate deceptive buzz-terms to various "target audiences," such as business leaders.

The same "packaging" technique is modified slightly to market ideas to children. How did Britney Spears and Eminem manage to become popular among 8-year-olds who are typically not yet sexually aware? By targeting a market. Targeting a market—that is, its "proper packaging"—helps ensure that it can be sold to and will be accepted by virtually any audience. Just as entertainers who look like prostitutes and drug addicts are sold to little children, politically charged curriculums are "marketed" to youngsters in the classroom, too. To do it, the "advertisers" (in this case, curriculum developers) must poll/test/survey the target subjects (including your kids) to find out what makes them tick. Then they know how to appeal to them, to "market" their politically correct wares.

Section 3.- CREATING A "PSYCHOLOGICAL ENVIRONMENT"

Wrongheaded legislation emerges from the fact that policymakers are convinced by professional manipulators that the majority of citizens—or at least the big political contributors—actually favor such initiatives as recycling, multiculturalism, wetlands "conservation" and graphic sex education. That is why paid provocateurs representing vested interests must generate their phony consensus from deceptive "lay" meetings—to dupe community members into believing they have input into the decision-making process.

Pupils in the classroom are similarly duped, via activities, discussion groups, "tests," surveys, and curricular materials designed not to teach, but to deceive—by appealing to the children's egos, by making them believe their gut reactions are real solutions to problems without reference to facts, research or timeless principles.

Creating and controlling the psychological environment requires the application of three axioms:

- **Repetition:** *If people hear the same phrases and slogans often enough, they will come to believe them, or at least accept them. They will rarely recall where the ideas originally came from.*
- **Isolation:** *If individuals are isolated, undermined, embarrassed, and out-maneuvered often enough, they will give up or become so irrational in the presentation of their views that no one who is not already in their camp will listen. This is also called marginalization*

and de-legitimizing the opposition. (This technique is frequently applied during Senate confirmation hearings.)

- **Labeling:** *If negative labels are applied consistently, both subtly and blatantly, to certain actions (such as faith in God) or to certain individuals and organizations (e.g., "Boy Scouts" or "Promise Keeper"), they can, by their very mention be made to function as negative conditioned responses.*

Commit these three tenets to memory: repetition, isolation and labeling. Their successful application produces a populace that values expediency and group approval over independent thought and knocks out considerations about right and wrong. The target population will actually work to avoid any appearance of individualism, for fear of being seen as a "maverick" in the eyes of the group. This goes a long way in quashing dissent. The goal of life becomes to hide in a social group, allowing organizational leaders to make the tough calls.

Moreover, "framing the debate" is key to keeping control of the psychological environment. When you frame the debate, you direct, or drive, the discussion; that is, you deflect attention from the real agenda. In effect, you tell people what they are going to think about and for how long.

Section 4.- SCHOOLS: LAUNCHPADS FOR INDOCTRINATION

I want to focus your attention on the classroom setting for just a moment, because this business about framing the debate and controlling the environment of thought begins in the elementary and secondary schools, then continues at the university, and on into public forums, committees and task forces, by which time the now-grown-up child is thoroughly immunized against logic and immersed in group-think.

Raw indoctrination, as used in the classroom, entails to a large extent framing the debate. Just as the media tends to dictate what American adults read, hear, discuss and think about, students in today's psychology-driven classrooms are encouraged toward activities that support a particular worldview. As soon as pupils begin to deviate from that worldview, the topic or activity is changed or ended.

This, of course, is the opposite of free expression and open discussion. But that's not how it is labeled. It is characterized as "academic freedom."

Indoctrination, like its sister, brainwashing, is a sophisticated form of psychological manipulation. Both go beyond framing the debate because their purpose is not only to redirect attention and disrupt the thought process, but to systematically *root out* a person's emotional support system. This is something that not only you, as an adult, must train yourself to recognize and combat, but you must teach your children to do so as well.

There are five basic steps to indoctrination:

1. Eradicate the subject's support base—his/her intellectual and emotional life raft. (Undermining family and religious tenets are just two favored approaches.)

2. Bombard the subject's senses with a steady diet of conflicting, confusing images and words in order to impair rational thought and discourage reflection (cognition). The technical term for this is "thought disruption." (The chaotic nature of the school day, with its non-stop interruptions, is a good example.) The result is a vacuum where a belief system used to be.

3. Once a vacuum has been created, leaving the subject vulnerable and impressionable (the technical term is "willing to receive stimuli"), lead the subject to the desired ideas, concepts, and beliefs via *trained intermediaries* (i.e., facilitators, "clinicians," change agents, agitators, marketing gimmicks).

4. Condition the subject through repeated exposure to the "desired" beliefs using a wide variety of formats and activities—i.e., repeat the lies until the targeted subject believes them.

5. Test, survey, or analyze market figures to ascertain whether the new beliefs have been internalized and accepted. If not, "recycle" the subject—i.e., go back to Step 1.

Indoctrination depends on the intermediary (in this case, a teacher trained as a change agent) appearing value-neutral even though the materials and the agenda are not. This is why the new breed of teacher is called a "coach," "clinician," "mentor," or (once again) "facilitator." Teachers are taught to avoid lectures, rote drills and workbooks, because instruction, as Baby Boomers (and older) knew it—i.e., "knowledge imparted in a systematic manner"—is not desired anymore. Rather, the intent is to interpose, or smuggle in, certain impressions, notions, attitudes, judgments and conclusions into the vacuum created by having stripped away the belief system and impaired rational thought. In this way, viewpoints that might have been rejected by pupil out of hand will appear plausible. The technical term for this type of "plausibility" is *internalization*. That is the essence of psychological manipulation.

Look at Step 4 again, conditioning: This means the target population group must experience repeated exposure to the same "desirable" beliefs using a wide variety of formats and activities and slapping the deceptive message on anything that stands still. This "message" can mean building support for global warming and "Smart Growth," moving notions about national sovereignty toward favoring an international criminal court system, or integrating homosexuality into the military so that a draft eventually has to be reinstated to keep troops.

For the sake of argument, let's take "acceptance of homosexuality." This can be promoted in a variety of ways: by (1) offering a Barbie doll knock-off called the "Gay Billy" doll, (2) working with producers to ensure that TV programs feature gay and lesbian characters in ever-more-graphic homosexual plot-lines, (3) handing out pro-homosexual literature to youngsters around elementary schools, (4) keeping the topic of homosexuality in the news, with always-sympathetic articles in popular magazines (gay "marriage," hate crimes, gay parades, etc.), and (5) launching non-stop ad and billboard campaigns, usually under the cover of AIDS awareness. In a classroom setting, conditioning would entail an interdisciplinary approach so that the topic is inserted into all curricular areas.

One reason traditionalists have fared so poorly is that we have failed to utilize a similar multi-disciplinary approach to "selling" our views, such as heterosexual marriage. We have no billboards on the highway or in the subway stations. There's little effort to recruit good script writers and lobby producers so that marriage is portrayed positively, no one at the elementary schools checking for people illicitly handing out literature, no massive effort to buy up or take over existing media outlets. When we *do* launch news outlets, we label ourselves "conservative" or "religious" so that our opposition doesn't have to do it for us. In short, we seem to have zero sense of strategy and consistently shoot ourselves in the foot.

The final phase of indoctrination is always testing, to be sure the "desirable" new values or beliefs are internalized and accepted by the public. In the case of both homosexual tolerance and "sexual freedom" (promiscuity), for example, experts would look at the sales figures for the "Gay Billy" dolls, as well as for the Austin Powers doll that squawks "Are you horny, Baby?" at the child who picks it up off the shelf.

Sales figures function as a "test." If test results are disappointing, it is time to "recycle"; which means repeating the 5-step indoctrination process again, usually with a more hard-hitting approach.

Eventually, resistance to sex-filled entertainment starts to sound silly. If the Austin Powers doll that squawks "Are you horny, Baby?" is deemed funny by most parents instead of gross, then that's success. The reason the method works is that the various marketing campaigns, or "lessons," bypass the conscious, intellectual mind and shoot directly for the more vulnerable subconscious that is the foundation of a person's feelings and emotions. It goes right for the gut. This is also what is "sold" to parents and other taxpayers as "critical thinking skills," whereas it is a direct intrusion into the child's belief system.

Schools and Group-Think

Not only will you have to deal in meetings and on committees with the specific attack strategies used against you by the professional manipulators inside the education establishment, you must teach your children the pitfalls of misleading rhetoric. This means you will need to explain, and frequently, how words can be put together to deceive. In the Age of Oprah, for example, you will have to explain what "privacy" means. In an era when every TV show has people divulging the most intimate details of their lives, a child cannot possibly be expected to know what's private if you don't explain it—little by little, not all at once—while at the same time encouraging him always to refer back to principle (i.e., moral benchmarks) when in doubt.

Remember that government school educators deliberately use peer pressure to promote group-think, and that peer pressure is another term for creating a "mob mentality." The side-effect is contempt for authority early-on in the child's life. That is why youngsters come home with claptrap about Mommy and Daddy ruining the planet and why they ignore parents' admonitions against sexual experimentation. The moral authority of parents has been undercut. Their peers are the boss!

Former school psychologist Steven Kosser advises parents to help children understand the concept of privacy early, but without causing a confrontation at school. He suggests parents say something like the following:

> "Honey, some time a teacher at school may ask you a question about yourself, or your mom, or your dad, or someone else in your house; or they may ask questions about how we run our household. If you would feel awkward, or embarrassed, if your answer were written on the chalkboard in front of the room for everybody to see, then that answer is private, and you shouldn't write or talk about it with anybody except your mom, your dad, your doctor or your minister, okay? Please be sure to tell me if anything like this ever happens so that I can talk to the teacher about it, okay?"

I would add the caveat: "If someone at school ever tries to pressure you to discuss or give out sensitive information, you can always just answer 'I don't know,' then wait till you get home and talk to Mom or Dad about it."

Section 5.- PRINCIPLES OF PSYCH-WAR

We have examined a few Principles of Psych-War. Let's continue by recalling the most basic axiom:

- **All warfare is based on deception.**

This means every kind of war, not just some wars. Thus, we see that as early as 476 BC, Chinese strategists understood that success in war, be it armed or psychological, depends upon the ability to confuse and delude while concealing one's true character, weaknesses, strong points, and intentions. ***This is not "lying," as in bearing false witness against one's neighbor.*** It is strategic deception, which is much different. It refers to personal demeanor, the way you conduct yourself, not to something you say or write down about somebody else that is knowingly false.

- **Always let your opponent know that an escape route is open so that they will flee. Show him/her that there is a road to safety, and so create in his/her mind that there is an alternative to losing all. Then strike.**

Let's consider the allusion to an "escape route" here. Our opponents have always given us an escape route. What do we "escape" to? Legitimacy. Acceptance. What is the price? Capitulation on issues more important to your adversary.

The road to "safety" is enticing bait on some issue of lesser importance to an adversary. For example, the Democrats used a phony budget agreement in 1999, allowing Republicans to save face with the public by claiming victory. But once Republicans seized this route, they were attacked from another direction.

- **An enemy may be conquered more easily if the appropriate conditions have been created.**

What are the "conditions" an adversary will create?

"Framing the debate" and controlling the psychological environment.

- **Recruit persons who are highly intelligent but can appear to be stupid; who may seem to be dull but are in reality strong; who are vigorous and energetic, but can appear to weary easily; who are well-versed in earthy matters and able to endure humiliation in order to succeed.**

This axiom is absolutely crucial to success, as we shall see once we get into a few actual battle scenarios. Again, this is not lying. In fact, you needn't say a word to pull this off.

- **Do not gobble preferred baits.**

Our opposition throws us a bone ("bait") every once in awhile on some pet issue and in the process saps our energies and diverts our attention from still other matters. Too often, we take the bait without a quibble, forgetting the old adage about picking one's battles carefully.

- **Weary your opponents by keeping them constantly occupied. Make them rush about by offering them ostensible advantages.**

How many times does this have to happen before we get the message? The abortion issue is a perfect example. We are kept so occupied with the murder of the unborn that we have nearly forgotten about the kids who are alive! Get it into your head that our adversaries' ***don't care*** about the unborn or the safety of mothers one way or the other. As long as the issue keeps us ***busy***, that's good news for them. If you don't believe it, go back and study the chronological history of the abortion debate, then juxtapose the various wins and losses pro-lifers have had on other issues in the House and Senate. Another example is race. We are so constantly confronted with articles and news centering on racial tension, that even with a black President, hardly anybody remembers original goal of a colorblind society.

- **Those skilled at making an opponent move do so by creating a situation to which s/he must conform—for example, by enticing him with something he is sure to take.**

This is what the opposition has done with declining school test scores. By creating a situation in which academic scores were ***sure*** to decline, we have been enticed by the bait of "school reform" and "standards," which we could be expected to take. From there, it is a short jump to restructuring schools, ostensibly to improve test results. Unfortunately, both the "standards" and the "reforms" are largely bogus. So, the terms were redefined, to our children's detriment.

- **Do not demand accomplishment of those who have no talent.**

This sounds laughable and obvious, but it isn't. For example, the staff advisor for education for most conservative Members of Congress too often has no particular expertise in that field or, for that matter, any knowledge concerning the major players and vested interests. Worse, the position tends to be viewed as a stepping-stone for political science majors barely out of college, toward something more exciting. Many such staffers are the sons or daughters of important Somebodies and are not exactly what you would call "quick studies." Much of the information that passes through these young staffers' hands, however, is critical to good policymaking. Yet, the extent of the staffer's knowledge about education is something along the lines that John Dewey was a saint who modernized the schools (slogan: "progressive education") and that the tax-free, left-wing lobbying union, the National Education Association (NEA), looks out for teachers and kids. The facts are that Dewey was a self-admitted socialist who insisted that transmission of knowledge was over-rated, and the NEA pushes an annual far-left agenda that barely touches on academic matters.

Only the most experienced and talented persons should hold such advisory positions. They should be well-paid so that it is clear that even though the position may be low-profile, it is highly valued. Our opponents have always known this and, therefore, hold the advantage.

- **Those skilled in war bring the opponent to the field of battle. They do not allow themselves to be taken or drawn there.**

Traditionalists and political conservatives always wind up debating issues on their adversary's turf. When we go to meetings, it is at a time and place of the opposition's choosing. When we debate in a public forum, it frequently is the big TV networks that gets us there—and guess whose agenda gets the positive coverage? Big Media, of course, is the bait, and we take it. When we invite our adversaries to debate us and our invited experts on our turf, what happens? They just blow us off.

- **Disrupt the opponent's alliances using deceptive operations: "Be seen in the west and march out of the east; lure your enemy to the north and strike in the south": Drive the opposition leaders crazy; bewilder them so that their constituencies disperse in confusion.**

We've already taken up how the counterculture Left drives us crazy with its double standards and hypocrisy. What we haven't discussed is *the element of surprise*. Our opponents have been masters of "luring" their quarry. Notice how our once-firm religious alliances, for example—the ones that supported us during and prior to the Reagan years—have "dispersed in confusion." Conservatives once believed they won the 2000 and 2004 elections, but the truth turned out less settling: Our alliances became disrupted. Many conservatives went to third parties, didn't vote at all, and continue to squabble among themselves, having become disoriented and disillusioned with the democratic process. Many of today's conservatives sound more and more like yesterday's progressives.

The allusion to "luring one's enemy to the north and striking in the south" means using the element of surprise—for example, by appearing to capitulate on some issues when really buying time to snatch a bigger prize. School privatization schemes like charter schools, for instance, will in the long run inject additional federal dollars into the system—along with more red tape. Big Government advocates knew this, but they played up a seeming capitulation on the issue of charter schools. But bureaucratic paperwork and oversight made the process of launching a private school almost prohibitive, sending tuitions sky high and cutting out even most of the upper-middle class.

When educrats appear to be withdrawing—for example, over the issue of vouchers or "scholarships" for poor students to attend private schools—remember that such ploys often are designed to draw out the opposition (to see who you are) and to create a false sense of security. Later, your enemy will deliver a decisive counterstroke that will neutralize you. The allusion to "luring" and then "striking" employs what I call the "dog bone" scenario: For example, in the 1990s, pro-lifers were lulled into the idea that they were seeing a "withdrawal" of sorts. Leftist legislators tossed us a bone on abortion for teenagers—a requirement for parental notification (which, predictably, is now the subject of lawsuits). A few months later, conservatives were shocked to discover that our adversaries were preparing to pass a bill protecting partial-birth abortion, something most folks had not even heard of at that time. In other words, they threw a bone to deflect attention from what they were really up to.

- **Numbers alone confer little advantage.**

Our opposition has been master of the numbers game, selecting the times and places for confrontation, packing audiences and committees, so they can count on their numbers being greater than ours. But remember, Jesus understood the principle that numbers are not the whole story: He had only 12 disciples, and they changed the world.

- **Agitate the masses and cause insurgencies.**

Remember Kent State? The Watts riots? The Million Mom March, etc. These mass temper tantrums serve not only to agitate, but to *distract*. Eventually, the tactic invites a police state due to its repetitive nature for every issue, running the gamut from angst over the Federal Reserve to "climate change."

- **Avoid the opposition when his spirit is keen and attack him when it is sluggish. This is control of the morale factor.**

Why do you suppose most school-issue-related meetings are held in the evenings? True, most people work during the day, but remember—change agents and facilitators are "working" days, too. But they know you'll be more sluggish in the evenings and plan accordingly.

- **When a faction's leaders or policies are inconsistent, spirits will be low and the rank-and-file angry. When people belonging to the faction continually gather in small groups and whisper, leaders have lost the confidence of their constituents.**

Our opponents sow confusion, start false tumors, publish misleading reports, slant statistics and survey data, then "reward" some conservatives with prized appointments—all aimed at creating discord among their adversaries. Once conservatives and traditionalists are busy denouncing each other, the culprits on the other side have won.

Section 6.- LOOSE LOGIC

The way in which the mind goes about drawing conclusions is based upon established patterns of logic. This is important if you want to avoid falling victim to "thought disruption."

Thought disruption is the inability to sustain a line of reasoning from its beginning to a conclusion. Sometimes the cause is continuous interruptions. The interruptions built into the typical school day have, for example, impaired children's ability to concentrate. Later, this is mistaken for a nonexistent psychological malady: Attention Deficit Disorder. The "deficit," of course, is the lack of learning time created by schools.

But there is another cause of thought disruption. Most people argue in such a way as to make their case appear stronger than it actually is. This serves to distract listeners; eventually both parties may even forget what they were talking about. This is especially relevant to environmental issues, as most people (including the extremists themselves) are not scientists and, therefore, do not participate in real scientific deliberations. Among the methods of falsely augmenting a case are:

- **cutting part of a quotation (misquoting or incompletely quoting)**
- **dismissing alternatives**
- **changing the subject**
- **exaggerating facts**

- **appealing to popularity**
- **smearing opponents**

Sometimes the mischief is done unintentionally, but not in the case of the professional. A "pro" knows better than to commit the errors we will be studying, although such a person may do it anyway because lay audiences today are not expected to be able to pick up on faulty reasoning.

A fallacy of logic is a deceptive maneuver intended to bolster an argument. Sometimes we deceive ourselves, so whether the fallacy was committed accidentally or on purpose is of little account. There are, of course, many fallacies, and we shall consider here the ones parents and other citizens are most likely to encounter:

-- oversimplification
-- hasty generalization
-- false analogy
-- false dilemma
-- hypothesis contrary to fact
-- misaligned cause-effect
-- circular reasoning
-- distraction
-- ill-defined terms

-- false appeals
 > the smear ("black PR")
 > appeal to expertise
 > "genetic" fallacy
 > appeal to fear
 > the straw-man argument
 > appeal to popularity
 > irrelevance
 > appeal to common practice

The Oversimplification

Let's take the oversimplification. This fallacy stems from the normal desire to impose orderliness on complex facts. Slogans are typical oversimplifications: "Go Green!" Banners and billboards often are mediums for slogans or sound-bites that oversimplify problems and sell ideas. Ads hyping the first attempts at "selling" a now-defunct term, outcome-based education (OBE), in the 1980s included, for example:

- **"All children can learn."**
- **"Success breeds success."**
- **"We need to create a level playing field."**

These three slogans functioned as sales pitches for OBE, and they are still heard today by educators who want to debunk the competitive model.

Slogans are easy to remember, contain only a few words—and vastly oversimplify the issue of learning. In responding to "all children can learn," you can innocently ask: "Are you saying that all people have identical abilities? That they can all learn the same things, sooner or later?"

In response to "success breeds success," you can ask: "How about apathy? Can success ever breed apathy?"

In response to Number 3—"We must create a level playing field," you can ask: "Can't leveling the playing field actually damage the self-esteem of those who would excel?"

By asking these questions in a non-confrontational way—think back to those basic Principles of Psych-War—which ones did these questions utilize? [*Think before responding.*]

Answers :

- **Framed the debate and created the "appropriate conditions" for battle.**
- **Laid the groundwork for controlling the psychological environment.**
- **Planted seeds of dissent and quietly bolstered weaker supporters.**
- **Made use of the indirect approach.**

Remember that your aim is to encourage all members of the group to question the presenter or provocateur, not to be labeled a "naysayer." *Posing counter-arguments in the form of questions often will plant seeds of doubt in the minds of other participants*, and that is what you want. If you have to do all the contradicting yourself, then you can also be easily isolated. It is helpful, of course, to have more than one vocal supporter asking the questions. For that reason, if you can manage it, try to avoid allowing either the provocateur or other group members to see you fraternizing, especially immediately prior to or after the meeting. Delphi-countering questions should appear spontaneous, coming from all over the room.

Another way to *avoid the "naysayer" label is to phrase your beliefs in positive, rather than negative, terms.* Instead of stating, for example, that you are against fornication, adultery, pornography, and illegitimacy, say that you are ***for*** sexual purity, marriage, uplifting art, and two-parent homes. Instead of saying you are against recycling—which often causes more energy to be consumed in collecting and reprocessing materials than is either feasible or prudent—say instead that you are ***for*** efficient cost-benefit ratios. And then explain what that means.

Instead of denouncing multicultural studies and diversity, assert that you are ***for*** accurate, chronological world history and foreign language courses that incorporate the geography, customs and culture of the country in question. Instead of decrying wetlands preservation at the expense of human needs, say that you are ***for*** a United States that has such bountiful crops and livestock reserves that it can afford to keep its citizens from hunger and something left over for the rest of the world. In other words, use the Left's own biases to your advantage.

Also try to use the negative interrogative form of phrasing a question; for example: "***Can't*** leveling the playing field actually damage self-esteem?" By saying "can't you" and "don't you" instead of "can you" and "do you," you win a small psychological advantage, because you are implying: "Of course you can't," and "of course you don't." This places your adversary on the defensive. (Next time you listen to a TV interview, especially one in which you know the interviewer will be hostile to the guest, count how many times that interviewer uses this technique.)

The Smear

Another fallacy is the smear. The smear can be blatant or exquisitely subtle. The smear, of course, is generally connected with the use of emotionally charged language and is not a technique to return in kind. In other words, if you return the favor, it will probably backfire.

The reason smears often work well for professional manipulators is because (a) they take pains to set up the smear beforehand, and (b) they know the right "hot buttons" ahead of time—that is, the terms and expressions that are sure to have the desired effect on the rest of the crowd. In many cases, they also have the media for backup. Professionals know that the media will repeat terms in the same manner the provocateur defines them and thus will perpetuate the ruse.

So, let's take a rather touchy example here: Let's talk about the term "cult." Now work with me here, because you're going to have to keep a really open mind, and there's a surprise at the end of this.

The dictionary defines "cult" simply as "devoted adherents." Yet, the term has come to connote fanaticism and weird ritualism. Thus the term has gained a negative reputation. The same is true of the words "fundamentalist" and "fundamentalism," beginning with the dual crises in Iran and Iraq from the mid-1970s to the present. Thus, it is no stretch for religion-bashers in America today to link the two terms, as in "fundamentalist cult."

The phrase "right-wing" is another hot-button term, even though its literal meaning has been changed from its fascist-Nazi origins to mean just about anything that is politically incorrect, especially "conservative."

Now we are going to string together all these terms: "conservative, right-wing fundamentalist cult." Surely you have heard this. Through repetition, a new phrase then emerged —"Christian, right-wing fundamentalist cult." Today, the phrase functions as a slogan.

Now, try this exercise: Remember the phrase from the old children's movie, "teenage mutant Ninja turtles"? Well, say it. [Repeat twice, out loud.] Now say "Christian, right-wing fundamentalist cult." Notice a familiar ring?

What you've got here is called a "meme"—a phrase that flows and is easily remembered, like "Cop Killers" and "love glove." If you want to understand the concept of memes further read my third book *CLONING OF THE AMERICAN MIND*, but the bottom line is that one can engineer a negative or a positive public reaction to something by using meme-like expressions that stick in the mind (which is why children like them).

So, let's continue with "Christian, right-wing fundamentalist cult."

Until recently, the term "fundamentalist" wasn't part of the American lexicon, possibly because "fundamentalism" in the context of the Muslim sects wasn't yet an issue. But once Islamic extremism and violence started being exported all over the world beginning in the 1980s, provocateurs were able to coin the terms "fundamentalist Christians" and "Religious Right." Although the term "orthodox Jews," for example, refers to those who practice strict adherence to Judaism, constant reminders of the Holocaust have so far kept "orthodox Judaism" from sliding into "fundamentalist Judaism," which would, of course, be taken for an insult. Nobody, however, says "orthodox Christian." Although occasionally you will hear "Greek Orthodox church" or "Russian Orthodox church," which refer specifically to denominations transplanted from Greece and Russia, respectively, there is no "Christian Orthodox Church" per se.

So, one way to neutralize the smear "fundamentalist Christian" is to say, "You must mean 'orthodox Christian', don't you?" Notice I added the "don't you" (i.e., the negative interrogative again) because that implies that the person who smeared you merely made a mistake. He or she can save face by admitting an error. You have given the provocateur "an escape route," as per Sun Tzu's Rules of Psych-War (review Section 5).

Now, the professional facilitator, or provocateur, may not resort to name-calling. Instead, s/he may use an ***implied*** smear, as demonstrated by the following (note: the portion in brackets can be filled in with something else):

- Even a child would see [that seat-time in a classroom doesn't equate to proficiency in subject matter].

- A person who really wanted to improve education [would agree that all children need a chance to succeed.]

- Everyone on the committee understands why [you are opposed to teaching about climate change].

- Even you would admit [that AIDS is a problem.]

Study these lead-in lines so you will learn to recognize implied smears in a hostile situation. In the first example above, you have been called "childish" by implication. In the second, you have been cast as a person who does not really want to improve education. In the third instance, you have been made the object of ridicule, a nut-case to be marginalized or ignored. In the last example, you have been called an extremist ("Even ***you*** would admit....")

The best way to approach a smear, then, especially if it is implied, as above, is to treat it as a distraction—another of the fallacies on the list (see below).

The Distraction

A distraction is an effort to divert people's attention from the real issue, in effect changing the subject or, in a group setting, get others to focus on something non-germane (such as you being a fundamentalist) as opposed to whatever is the issue at hand. Therefore, *it will remain your constant task to remember what it is, specifically, you are arguing about or discussing.*

This sounds easy and obvious, but it isn't. For example, if you are talking about funding for schools, the real issue may actually be narrower than school funding. It might be a curriculum, teacher salaries, new buildings, additional buses, after-school sports, adding psychologists and counselors, or more surveying and testing. All these are funding issues—some of which you may not want or need. *You absolutely must nail down the specific topic you want to discuss to keep control of the debate and avoid being trapped into a non-germane issue.*

Look back at the first lead-in for an implied smear on the preceding bulleted list: *"Even a child would see that seat-time in a classroom doesn't equate to proficiency in subject matter."* You not only have been called childlike, but everything that goes along with that—such as naïve and inexperienced. An appropriate response might be:

"Well, perhaps children don't have the maturity to understand that indulging in a lot of frantic activity doesn't necessarily equate to proficiency."

Then proceed to address the subject, which, in this case is what? The term "proficiency in subject matter." What does that really mean? In your outrage at having been called childish, you may have forgotten that your interpretation of proficiency is quite different from the provocateur's. So, without hesitating, you should respond in a pleasant tone of voice with something like this: "I will concede that in the past seat-time frequently has translated to social promotion, and endless repetition without any remedial help. But I do not agree that the present policy replaces seat-time for real, measurable results...."

The thing you must not do is to stop the discussion by allowing the group to be diverted from the subject to the charge of "childish." Ignore it. Move on.

Another approach is humor, as long as the accusation is direct and the situation is in a group setting, not a one-on-one confrontation. For example, suppose a facilitator, or even another member of the group, says to you:

• *"Even a right-wing Fundamentalist would admit [that seat-time in a classroom doesn't equate to proficiency in subject matter.]"*

You should respond with something like:

• *"Yeah, I know our friend here just called me a wacko right-wing Bible-thumper. She would probably call Mother Theresa a cultist. But before we get too carried away with all this stereotyping, let's get back to the subject at hand which, I believe, was ...."*

And then continue with your views on proficiency. Under no circumstances, even if you're an atheist, should you deny the charge the attacker has made about being a right-wing Fundamentalist. Why? Because you don't want to come from a defensive position. If you do, you will never be permitted to discuss the real issue under consideration. All your time, and the time of the other group members, will be taken up arguing religion and/or religious bias. The term "right-wing Fundamentalist" is bait, pure and simple, and as per the Principles of Psych-War, you *"never take the bait."* One might add, *"never proceed from a defensive position."*

The next example is a little tougher:

- *"A person who really wanted to improve education [would agree that all children need a chance to succeed.]"*

To the uninitiated, this sounds reasonable. The smear, again, is by implication, but it's even more than that. In fact, this is a very versatile attack. But it is also tricky, because inasmuch as you have not been labeled outright, you run the danger of looking stupid if you jump to the bait and say something to the effect that you "do *so* care about improving education." The opposition's comeback to such a defensive remark would undoubtedly be: "Mr. Smith, I don't recall having said that *you,* specifically, didn't care about improving education."

Another poor response would be the question: "And what kind of person would *not* want to improve education?"

Normally a question puts your attacker on the spot. But **you don't want to give this person a forum**. Best to defuse the attack and move on. So here's another principle to remember: *"Don't give the opposition a forum."*

A good response to this smear is an easily memorized catch-all:

Provocateur: "A person who really wanted to improve education [would agree that all children need a chance to succeed.]"

Parent (You): "That makes sense."

And say it in a completely neutral tone of voice.

Now, you may be wondering: Why should I agree with this jerk? Because, by implication, you are also denying that you are "the person" the jerk is referring to. For the moment, you have defused a hostile situation and bought yourself time to think.

The provocateur has to change tactics. Either s/he has to change the subject entirely and accuse you then and there of being against educational reform, which would make the provocateur look worse than you, or s/he has to get back to the subject. So, let's try this again:

Provocateur: *"A person who really wanted to improve education [would agree that all children need a chance to succeed.]"*

You: *"That makes sense. The problem is deciding the form which that "chance" should take."*

Provocateur: (Long silence.)

You see, there's really no smart-mouth comeback the provocateur can make to your comment. S/he has no choice but to debate your issue.

Now let's take a harder fallacy: the hypothesis contrary to fact. A hypothesis is a theory. A theory must be supported by a variety of factual data, and must also contain counter-arguments, which are factual as well. The provocateur who tries to get a group to go along with something most people don't really believe will invariably present a theory without acknowledging any counter-arguments.

Take, for example, "climate change," "global warming," or whatever the label-of-the-week happens to be. Although there is considerable debate among scientists as to whether there has been any rise in the planet's temperatures (some findings show them actually falling instead of rising), and even though the small tenths of a percentage point showing a rise of temperature in some localities can be attributed to cyclical factors (having gone up and down repeatedly).

Following Hurricanes Katrina and Rita in 2005, news anchors commented that "scientists are now wondering just how much global warming is responsible for these monster storms we've been having…."

But after a hacker broke into the computers at the University of East Anglia's Climate Research Unit (CRU) in 2009 and released 61 megabytes of confidential files into the Internet, that was pretty much the final nail in the coffin for global warming. Skeptics finally got some respect. Those who took the time to examine the files—which included some 1079 emails and 72 documents—found it unsurprising that CRU might have wanted to keep them under wraps. As Australian writer Andrew Bolt, of Melbourne's *Herald Sun* and Sydney's *Daily Telegraph*, put it, this scandal could well be "the greatest in modern science." The e-mails between NASA scientists, publicized in 2010, pretty much confirms Mr. Bolt's assessment.

Nevertheless, newscasters and other vested interests continue to perpetuate disinformation about global warming, and legislators are bent on redistributing America's wealth via such deceptive laws as Cap-and-Trade (gratefully stalled in the Senate in July 2010, with no doubt variations of it to come). The message to federal agencies, including schools, is clear: Get onboard with global-warming malarkey or lose your funding.

Thus, it is the job of true scientists and other "refuseniks" to find ways to pique the curiosity of the masses and to generate a healthy skepticism among those, such as parents of schoolchildren, who continue to be victimized by the hoax. The terms "how bad" and "the monster storms we've been having" are the deceitful keys here. The implications are that (a) global warming is a fact, not a theory, and (b) the phrase "we've been having" suggests that "monster storms" are a recent phenomenon—i.e., a first-time-ever event, or at least a rare event, which they are not.

Because most folks focus on their own experience, and not on esoteric scientific arguments, they are likely to see only the damage to their own house, neighborhood and country, and therefore miss both the larger issue—and any deceptive language. So, when President George W. bush refused to sign an environmental agreement like the Kyoto Protocol, unthinking and preconditioned Americans reacted to this news with the "appropriate" degree of outrage—even though the agreement would negatively impact every person in the United States, provide no long-term gains for Third World nations, and have zero effect on hurricanes or any other climate phenomenon.

That is one reason I tend to go back repeatedly to education, the schools and the negative impact of mandated group-think. Parents, of course, are the first educators and should be the primary educators, too—in a perfect world. If parents do not place a premium on independent thinking and principle, then children probably will not pick up on it either. This places the republic very much at risk, because the America of the Founders was very much predicated on an education based on a common base of factual knowledge, on a sound foundation of principles, and on freedom of ideas, speech and conscience. None of these can flourish in an atmosphere of political correctness enforced through peer pressure and fear of alienation. To expect liberty to thrive and sustain itself under these conditions is folly.

Section 7.- LET'S PLAY "TRUMP THE FACILITATOR"

In this section you will study various scenarios that have occurred somewhere in the United States. You will see how provocateurs twist your views to their advantage—and learn how to stop them from doing so. We will try out various methods—from downright lousy responses to mediocre attempts to superlative comebacks. So let's start off easy with **Scenario #1**.

Provocateur: "Everyone on the committee understands why [you are opposed to teaching about condoms.]"

Now, a provocateur will make this comment either in a patronizing tone, as if talking to a child, or in a harsh, attack-mode. Either way, the purpose is to demoralize you. Remember, the smear is not blatant; it is implied—the idea being, *there's something wrong with you, and that the rest of the group should, therefore, ostracize you.*

Consequently, you must not take the bait by making a retort like Jane here is going to do:

Jane: "If you're implying I'm a Christian fundamentalist, and using that as the sole reason for my objections to classroom demonstrations of condoms, then you are not only being a bigot, but you're trying to taint every objection to suit yourself."

Now, what Jane said may well be the case. *But she must not say it.* If she does, the provocateur will smile knowingly and maintain control. Jane may even be booed out of the room unless more than half the people on the committee not only share her views, but are specifically Christians. Mob mentality, remember? As in the reaction to the word "cult," people are going to distance themselves from Jane in order to save themselves.

Another equally poor retort is demonstrated by George:

> **George:** "Whaddya mean, 'everyone understands?' I resent the implication that there is something wrong with my point of view and I resent your patronizing me."

What's wrong with this response? [*Think before continuing*.]

[Answer:] George is arguing. *Arguing with a facilitator merely piles a distraction on top of a distraction.* So, let's try this again, with Ginger.

> **Provocateur:** "Everyone on the committee understands why [you are opposed to teaching about condoms.]"
>
> **Ginger:** "How nice of everyone. I'm touched."

Then, she looks directly at the facilitator, smiles and says: "It is a credit to your leadership that this kind of team spirit has been generated."

Now ***that*** is a discussion-stopper. The provocateur's attempted smear will be so transparent as to hit everyone between the eyes. Ginger has maintained polite neutrality and thanked everyone for their good manners. Depending on your ability to stay composed and your skill at judging the limits of what you can get away with, you can have fun with this. After the inevitable silence (and don't let silence throw you by suddenly looking down or sideways; instead, maintain eye contact with the facilitator), Ginger could continue by adding something like:

> **Ginger:** "Now, if we might, I'd like to go back to the topic of our discussion, [the problem with spending time on condom demonstrations.]"

The good news in this exchange is that Ginger has "outed" both the provocateur and the smear. She returned the provocateur to the subject.

Now let's see what this would sound like in another situation:

> **Provocateur:** "Even a right-wing Fundamentalist will admit AIDS is a problem."
>
> **Debra:** "You're right. AIDS is a problem. The question is should the problem of AIDS be addressed by a six-year-old?"

Debra has forced the provocateur to get back to the subject by refusing to play the game.

Moreover, smears can be handled both as stereotyping and distractions. One way to recognize the smear tactic is that your specific statements, arguments, or principles *are never addressed*. The targeted individual or group is instead attacked for what he/she/it supposedly represents.

Let's move on to **Scenario 2,** this one between Parent and a School Board Member. In this scenario, we're going to take up a fallacy known as *irrelevance*. It's a variation of the distraction—the insertion of irrelevancies, to distract everyone, once again, from the topic at hand. Here's a typical exchange you might hear at a school board meeting:

Parent: I think sex education ought to be scrapped. It desensitizes a personal subject, much of the information itself is wrong-headed, and the kids don't learn anything worthwhile.

Board Member: That's a little extreme, don't you think? It's the responsibility of society to see that children learn about sex. Surely you'll agree that children need information that doesn't come off the street.

Parent: Of course, but the schools are not providing that.

Board Member: Sex is a very important topic and an integral part of life. Don't you think that sex is important for every child?

Parent: Of course, it's important. That's why the schools shouldn't teach it!

Parent isn't falling for the bait here. Parent is not going to let that Board Member draw her into an irrelevant conversation about *the responsibility of society* or *whether sex is an integral part of life*. Board Member is going to have to talk about Parent's topic—propriety and age-appropriateness—not the subject of the Board's choosing.

Let's try an irrelevancy argument that's a little harder: **Scenario 3** is between a facilitator and another average parent.

Parent: A budget agreement that calls for even more federal funding for education is absolutely wrong-headed. No matter how much money is appropriated, it is never enough, and too much is spent on non-academic matters.

Facilitator: But it is vital that children have state-of-the-art equipment to be well-educated in this day and age, and that's expensive. This is the Information Age, after all.

Parent: High-technology is no more vital to elementary reading, spelling, addition and subtraction than a lamp shade.

Facilitator: High-technology is vital to everyone. Don't you have a computer at home?

Parent: What's that got to do with it?

Facilitator: Well, don't you think most children will also need to use one?

Parent: You give the impression that high technology is the primary thing school districts are spending money on. That is hardly the case. I am talking about concentrating first on basic fundamental curriculum, which is getting short shrift with or without a computer.

Facilitator is losing this battle, too, even though Parent did misstep. Can you tell how Parent almost goofed? [*Think before continuing*.]

Answer: Parent implied that basic subjects do not require a computer. While that is true in the first three grades, basic subjects today can be enhanced via the use of computers and the Internet. Fortunately, Facilitator probably is busy concentrating on the Information Age and is about to deflect attention from the issues of basic subject areas. Parent forced Facilitator back to the topic at hand by subtly reminding everyone of the topic—which was what? [*Think before continuing*. Don't peak ahead at the answer.]

Answer: Education's budgetary priorities.

Now let's try a more difficult distraction:

Here's the situation: The local housing authority at the County level is placing a drug abuser rehabilitation center (halfway house) in an upper-middle-class suburb. Angry residents converge upon the town meeting in force, waving a report that states property values are already depressed by 30 percent. The housing authority calls the report invalid, stating that there is in fact no drop in house prices because real estate agents say that houses are selling like hot cakes, even better than they did last year and three years ago. Is anything wrong here? [*Think before continuing.*]

Answer: Yes, something is wrong. The housing authority has changed the subject. The subject was changed to *pace of sales* instead of the one residents were angry about—*depressed property values*. Indeed, the lower property values (house prices) could be the reason for brisk sales! People that once could not afford a house in the neighborhood can now do so. So, while both parties are discussing houses, the housing authority is using irrelevant facts not related to the argument to rebut the residents' outcries.

Actually, this scenario represents two fallacies, irrelevance and an appeal to expertise. In trying to counter a County "expert," or "authority," most people take a subservient position. The professional title of the "expert" intimidates people, even those who may be experts themselves in some other field. Too often, we are afraid to question the "authority" of an expert and think we are somehow just not following the argument. If, while listening, you have the nagging feeling that something is wrong with an expert's argument, something probably is.

In **Scenario 4**, we'll address the *straw-man argument*. Basically, a straw-man argument is one in which a position is attacked when there is no one around to defend it. A non-existing or non-present entity is attacked, so there is little chance of being proved wrong. Exaggeration and distortion are typical giveaways. Take the following exchange between Gregory and Patty.

> **Gregory:** "What do you make of those 8,000 parents in Texas who kept their kids out of the National Assessment on test day?"
>
> **Patty:** "I think they're a bunch of nuts who want to run the school system."
>
> **Gregory:** "How so?"
>
> **Patty:** "Teachers and administrators should have a say in how the school is run. Throwing out all the tests just because you don't like multicultural studies or something is crazy."
>
> **Gregory:** "Well, I don't think they should throw all the tests out, either."

OOPS! Gregory fell into it. He bought into Patty's straw-man argument. Where did things start to go wrong for Gregory? [*Think.*]

Things start getting out of whack when Gregory asks "how so?" Patty is entitled to her opinion that the 8,000 parents in Texas are "a bunch of nuts," but she's on thin ice about their wanting to run the school system. *Since none of the 8,000 parents is present, there is no one to challenge that assumption.* Gregory should have nailed Patty on it.

Then it gets worse. *Does every one of those 8,000 parents want to do away with all tests?* They may have protested the National Assessment, but that's a far cry from "every test." Perhaps these disgruntled parents simply are protesting the National Assessment.

A question to ask yourself when confronted with arguments in which the target has no way of responding: How many of the accused really hold that opinion? If you can't tell, you are probably facing a straw-man argument.

Most of the pamphlets and handout materials given to teachers and the public by the National Education Association, the Education Commission of the States, People for the American Way, and other radical groups rely on straw-man arguments. None of the people the materials attack can possibly defend their positions if they aren't present and if their side is not presented in the literature.

Let's move along to **Scenario 5**: the *distorted argument*. A distorted argument is one that distracts everyone by emotionalizing the discussion. Here we have a grades-free, "child-centered," non-competitive educational proponent and on the other side, a traditionalist who believes in the competition, excellence model.

> **Child-Centered Learning (CCL) Proponent:** "Grades should be discouraged. Every student should progress at his or her own pace. They should either pass or get remedial help. That way no child will be pressured by

senseless competition but instead will be encouraged to just understand the material."

Traditionalist: "Let's just let kids stay in their fourth grade math classes until they're 30 years old!"

CCL Proponent: "Come on. I didn't say that a pupil should stay in one class indefinitely, I just think grades are counter- productive."

Traditionalist: "How do you expect this nation to be competitive if children never compete for anything?"

CCL Proponent: "What are you getting so uptight about? I don't want to do away with all competition; I just think making school subjects boil down to grades is a mistake."

Traditionalist: "Competitiveness is key to our economy. When you undercut the competitive urge, you risk this nation's economic survival, unless you're so in love with the idea of interdependence that you've lost interest in economic survival."

CCL Proponent: "Who said anything about interdependence? You're twisting everything I'm saying."

Time out! You may agree with our **Traditionalist**, but his argument is a mess. His point about the length of time the no-grade idea would add to the learning process may be humorous, and even effective with some members of the group. But because **Traditionalist**'s position becomes so exaggerated, it will be a turnoff to most members of the group and sound cynical. **Traditionalist**'s argument is also an oversimplification. A more reasoned comeback would be something like this:

Good Response for Traditionalist: "This sounds like an updated version of the 1970s 'readiness' concept—the idea that kids will understand the material as they become mature enough, or 'ready.' This is inconsistent with life and unduly prolongs the education process. People don't have an infinite amount of time to 'get' things in real life. And if they did, there wouldn't be incentive to make the extra effort. Grades provide that incentive and for that reason simulate real life."

With a response like that, you provide *rational* criticism. You rebut the no-grades argument without resorting to exaggeration, distortion, or cryptic remarks. You also utilize a favorite theme of liberals—making education more consistent with real life.

Now, on to **Scenario 6.** Watch how this exchange between Lynn and Brett actually invites an attack by distorting the issue and results in generalizations based on that distortion.

Lynn: "I think all these self-esteem curriculums are garbage."

Brett: "What do you mean?"

Lynn: "Well, for example, inventing historical facts to pump up African-American egos. According to the Afrocentric curriculums cited by Mary Lefkowitz, a respected scholar of classical Greek literature and history, the roots of Western civilization are in Africa; Egypt was supposedly a black African civilization whose philosophy and achievements formed the foundations of Western civilization; Napoleon deliberately shot off the nose of the Sphinx to alter its facial features so people wouldn't know it was African; Socrates and Cleopatra were black (Cleopatra supposedly was described as 'black' in a chapter of Acts in the Bible); and the first human life, religion, philosophy, science, and mathematics came out of black Africa. Yet, as Lefkowitz points out, Cleopatra is not even mentioned in Acts and, in fact, died some 60 years before that book of the Bible was even written. Greek wives and mistresses were preferred, so ancient writers would not have hesitated to record that Cleopatra had an African ancestor if she really had had one."

Brett: "Well, when you put it that way, the Afrocentric program seems a little off-base.

Lynn: "Like I said, all this self-esteem nonsense is absolutely nuts."

Brett: "Hold it. I agree with you on the example you gave. But I didn't say I thought all self-esteem was nuts. Surely Afrocentric curriculums don't make up the entire self-esteem movement!"

Lynn started off well. Her hypothesis was broad and could have been knocked down if she hadn't offered reputable examples relating directly to the subject of self-esteem (which **Brett** obviously hadn't read).

But then **Lynn** generalized. Emotion got the best of her. She distorted her own argument in a misguided effort at enhancing it, and tried, in effect, to stick words in **Brett**'s mouth. She wound up in a fight instead of an intelligent discussion.

Now, for the sake of argument, let's try **Scenario 7** again. Let's pretend that, instead of *agreeing* with **Lynn** about Afrocentric curriculums being "off-base," **Brett** had responded differently, beginning from the point where **Lynn** says: "Like I said, all this self-esteem stuff is nuts ....":

> **Brett:** "Hey, don't you think it's unethical to demoralize kids in school?"
>
> **Lynn:** "Who said anything about demoralizing kids? That's another subject. Demoralizing someone means going out your way to embarrass and belittle a person."
>
> Now, it's Brett's comment about demoralizing kids that's the distraction. He says it to avoid addressing the examples on Afrocentric curriculums that Lynn gave to back up her objections to self-esteem. So even though Lynn may end up, in this case, having to qualify her statements about all self-esteem being "nuts," she may well win the argument because Brett wouldn't give her credit for her examples on Afrocentric curriculum.

Coming up is an example of a distortion you might hear after a PTA meeting. **Scenario 8** is an exchange between Marta and Dan. Watch how this conversation gets completely out of hand.

> **Marta:** "Not one penny more should be spent by taxpayers on education."
>
> **Dan:** "I suppose we ought to just let our kids grow up illiterate, right?"
>
> **Marta:** "Don't be absurd. I'm not anti-education. I just don't think existing funding is being used wisely or in the best interests of children."
>
> **Dan:** "Look, if we don't have a strong education system, our democracy is going to go down the drain. "

> **Marta:** "Okay! Lighten up. I didn't say anything about eliminating education. I just think the price tag is way out of synch with the results."
>
> **Dan:** "You know, I'm sick and tired of all these attacks on the public schools. Whenever you give public education short shrift, you lay the ax at the roots of democracy. Unless you don't think a democracy requires people to be educated . . ."
>
> **Marta:** "Oh, for Pete's sake. You're completely distorting what I said. I never said anything about not wanting kids to be educated or that education wasn't important to democracy."

This conversation is going nowhere. Dan is not at all interested in what Marta is saying. Dan has changed the subject, distorted Marta's comments, and implied that Marta is typical of *all* critics of public education—none of whom are there to defend either Marta's or their own positions. The usual cause of mistakes like the ones Marta made is over-emotionalism and not enough well-considered facts to bolster a viewpoint.

In **Scenario 9**, we're going to take up *circular reasoning*. Circular reasoning, also known as "begging the question" occurs when *the reason given for something sounds just like the question*; that is, the reason presupposes whatever one is trying to prove. Look at this simple example:

> **Question:** What makes you think that just because this curriculum is government-backed it is useful or appropriate for the classroom?

Response: The curriculum comes out of the National Diffusion Network, and everything in there is screened by a government-appointed board.

What's wrong with this response? [*Think before continuing.*]

Answer: It doesn't matter that the Board is appointed. No one mentioned appointments being independent of government (which they generally are not).

Now, suppose the respondent had left it at: "Because the curriculum is screened by the National Diffusion Network." Obviously if most members of a group do not know what the National Diffusion Network is—or that the government sponsors it—this comment will pass muster. It pays, therefore, to be well-informed.

In **Scenario 10** we have a harder version. Don't be put off by the volatile nature of this subject, which we're going to run through in two different ways.

(NOTE: This example may be inappropriate for children.)

Parent: "These curriculums on homosexuality are wrong, destroy morals, undercut parental teachings, and have no place in the public schools."

Principal: "Why do you say that?"

Parent: "Because it runs counter to the Bible."

Principal: "That's a pretty narrow view. What makes the Bible an authority on curriculum?"

Parent: "The Bible is the inspired word of God and it specifically condemns homosexuality, that's why."

Now, Parent's heart may be in the right place, but definitely not her argument. Why? [*Think before continuing*.]

Answer: Because it's obvious in this exchange that Principal is not at all impressed by the Bible, or he wouldn't have asked what made the Bible an authority. So the fact that the Bible condemns homosexuality is not going to sway him. Parent's argument comes across as circular reasoning.

So, let's try this again. (**Scenario 10-revised**)

> **Parent:** "These curriculums on homosexuality are wrong, destroy morals, undercut parental teachings, and have no place in public schools."
>
> **Principal:** "Why do you say that?"
>
> **Parent:** "Because most religious and ethical systems running back for thousands of years of civilization have taught that homosexuality demeans the human spirit, is physically and emotionally harmful, and not in the best interests of society."
>
> **Principal:** "Well, there's a lot of argument today on those points."
>
> **Parent:** "Exactly. That's why young children should not be getting curriculums that bolster one view. In fact, given the immense debate surrounding the causes and ramifications of homosexuality, the entire subject is inappropriate for children."

Hooray for Parent! The Principal's own argument has been used against him, and he is left with little to say, except maybe "I disagree."

Now let's throw in another possibility. Suppose, instead, Principal had responded with something like this:

> **Principal:** "Well, kids are maturing a lot faster these days, and that makes homosexuality an appropriate topic for the schools."

What is wrong with this logic?

Actually, Principal has made a typical mistake with this remark. Examine the following two sayings:

- *"People live longer today."*
- *"People have longer life spans today."*

Which is true, the first or the second, or both? [*Think.*]

Answer: Only the first one is true. The human life span has not changed in thousands of years. Copious records attest to life spans of 85 or even a little over 100, dating back from the time of Confucius. But there are no 500-year-old people. What has changed is that, proportionally, more people are living to those ages between 85 and 100, thanks to medical technology. In countries without such technology, fewer people live to these ages, of course. But to say that there is some new development producing 200-year-olds, for example, is without basis. Principal's argument about youngsters maturing earlier these days is similarly flawed.

Here's a comeback you can use for this kind of flawed argument to bolster your views against sex education and pro-homosexuality curriculums:

> **You:** "Are children really more mature today? That's a pretty sweeping generalization: Just because youngsters can draw

more spectacular pornographic pictures on their desks, or because they know more four-letter words than you and I did as youngsters, hardly makes them "mature." Girls in the Middle East, Latin America, and Asia typically have started menstruating at younger ages than white Anglos, and thus puberty is now changing among whites, too, due to intermarriage. But secondary sex characteristics do not translate to maturity of judgment, and many nations used to be aware of that, by being careful, for example, that young girls were chaperoned. I challenge you to come up with any evidence that American children or youngsters anywhere, are demonstrating maturity earlier now than they ever did."

Now we'll take up the *False Hypothesis*. A hypothesis is an unproven theory, pure conjecture or an educated guess. But no matter how "educated" the guess, it cannot be used to draw a conclusion unless there is something to support it, to make it credible. Frequently, the theory or assumption contains a kernel of truth but, just as frequently, those kernels are grossly exaggerated or biased. They don't support the conclusion drawn from them. If two theories, or "educated guesses," are paired with each other—"this plus that means such-and-such"—it is hard for you to interrupt and say, "wait a minute, the two things you just said don't go together." The two may even contradict each other. Then, there's the problem of any supportive evidence being highly questionable.

So: the variations on the false hypothesis theme are:

false cause **dubious evidence**
misaligned cause-effect **contradictory argument**
biased argument

Recognize that most "therefore"-type arguments come in a format that looks like one of these:

reasoning (or supportive evidence)

Hypothesis (theory or "given") -------------------->> conclusion

Or:

reasoning (or supportive evidence)

Cause -->> effect

Every theory is based on one or more assumptions, or "givens." If the assumption or "given" is false, off the subject, biased, or exaggerated, then the conclusion will suffer accordingly.

Professional provocateurs, as well as amateurs, often begin with mistaken or deliberately misleading statements that are in reality assumptions, or guesses. They dive right into the conclusion, possibly offering a lot of extraneous "reasons," before anyone can challenge them on their opening assumptions.

If you are quick, you may be able to stop them cold on their assumptions, but more often than not, it is a better approach to wait and let them finish. *The important thing is to keep your attention fixed on that first assumption or hypothesis*. While the ensuing reasoning may be equally poor and contain numerous inconsistencies, ***if you can challenge that first wrong assumption, or hypothesis, you will be ahead of the game.***

Sometimes, however, the "effect" simply does not logically follow the "cause." The key to nailing this variation on the false hypothesis is to come up with a different reasonable "cause" or assumption. For example, suppose Mr. or Ms. Facilitator says:

"Since the cause of AIDS and sexually transmitted diseases (STDs) is lack of protection during intercourse, kids should learn early to use a condom, and condoms should be made easily available through the school's health clinic."

Where is the "given" or hypothesis in the above statement? [*Think before continuing*.]

Answer: ***The cause of AIDS and STDs is lack of protection during intercourse.***

If the facilitator had changed just one word—"***A*** cause of AIDS" instead of "***The***" cause of AIDS—then the statement would have been harder to refute: *That one small change means allowances have been made for other possible causes, which gives you a wedge to offer another viewpoint.*

So, let's take version Number 1 first:

> **Facilitator:** "Since the cause of AIDS and sexually transmitted diseases (STDs) is lack of protection during intercourse... "

Your response in this instance must be aimed directly at the hypothesis, or assumption, like this:

> **Best Response:** "I question your assumption. The cause of AIDS and sexually transmitted diseases is promiscuous sex and dirty needles used by drug abusers. The cause is risky conduct. Therefore, the best 'protection' during intercourse is monogamy or abstinence."

Now you have forced Facilitator to focus on *your* topic (cause of AIDS and STDs), not *his* topic (condoms).

However, had Facilitator used Version Number 2, ***"A cause of AIDS and sexually transmitted diseases (STDs)…, "*** then you would go after Facilitator 's reasoning and conclusion, being sure to draw attention to the fact that the facilitator qualified his own hypothesis, like this:

> **Best Response:** ***"I will grant you that one cause of AIDS and sexually transmitted diseases is lack of protection during intercourse, but how does legitimizing promiscuous behavior and pretending that condoms are infallible reduce the activity that is primarily responsible for these health hazards? Doesn't your approach imply acceptance of unhealthy lifestyles that produce irresponsible behavior?"***

Again, Facilitator will have to focus on your topic—curbing promiscuous behavior—not on so-called his "safe sex" propaganda. Notice in the last sentence of this response, we have used the negative-interrogative form of the verb again, which confers upon your argument a psychological advantage.

This is what is known as "framing the debate." With a response like the two above, you give the rest of the group something different to think about. Without talking down to anyone, you have made them question the acceptance of unhealthy lifestyles. If Facilitator insists on returning to the topic of condoms—say, by giving statistics on reduced instances of HIV transmission using condoms—your comeback should be:

> **Comeback:** "What makes you think that promiscuous people are going to bother with condoms? In the past three years alone there have been numerous reports proving that homosexuals and promiscuous teenagers are

not moved by scare stories on AIDS and STD statistics, and that one in four teenage girls has an STD."

Now let's go a step further in this discussion of condoms, embarrassing as it may be. After all, one of the facilitator's best trump cards is embarrassment.

The most likely retort for a proponent of graphic sex education and/or condom distribution at this juncture, if he can't debate statistics and won't debate lifestyles, may be the old standby—raging hormones! In **Scenario 11**, a Health Clinic representative will debate a Parent.

Health Rep: "Look, we're talking about raging hormones here. There's no point in injecting pious morality into this."

Parent: "In other words, their instincts: As though they have no control over their behavior."

Health Rep: "I told you I wasn't going to debate morality. We are talking about *drives* that are common to all animal species."

Parent: **"**If that is so, then perhaps you can explain to me why all the "other animals" don't *need* condoms."

Is that a sure-fire conversation-stopper or what? Notice **Parent** *didn't suggest that animals can't get AIDS or STDs*. Researchers seeking cures inject experimental animals with various viruses to induce or simulate diseases, so you don't want to imply that animals absolutely can't get STDs, even though the possibility is remote in the natural environment. What you have to do is to foil two favorite beliefs of the condom crowd:

- That humans are just advanced forms of animals with no higher calling.

- That condoms are a viable option to preventing AIDS and STDs.

A word of warning, however, to emphasize the necessity of practicing the techniques presented here: Don't play around with the wording on this example. If, under stress, you had said: ***"Then perhaps you can explain to me why animals don't <u>use</u> condoms"*** instead of ***"... why animals don't <u>need</u> condoms,"*** the entire group would have dissolved into gasps of laughter and the meeting might even adjourn. I leave the obvious comeback to the reader's tender imagination.

Let's move along in our list of fallacies to Scenario 12 and the ***misaligned cause-effect:***

> **Example:** "Verbal scores on the Scholastic Achievement Test (SAT) have plummeted by "x" percent, while hours spent watching TV have soared by "y" percent. Therefore, TV watching is the cause of poor SAT performance."

Now, there probably is a correlation between hours spent watching TV and poor performance in school, and therefore on SAT scores as well. But stated this way, it is a fallacy, and can be torn down. Why? Because other reasonable factors *besides watching TV* can easily be substituted: poor teaching methodology, de-emphasis by schools on academics (as opposed to social concerns), lowered expectations, and so on. If the last sentence in speaker's comment had contained a qualifier —***"Therefore, TV watching <u>may be</u> a cause of poor SAT performance,"*** instead of ***"<u>is</u> the cause of poor SAT performance"***—there would have been grounds for a legitimate debate.

With this in mind, let's think about this often-heard remark:

"Inadequate information about sex results in unwanted teen pregnancy."

What's wrong with that statement? How can you knock it down? [*Think.*] Notice that in this instance the "effect" is placed at the beginning and the "cause" at the end. It doesn't matter, however, that the format is inverted. You still have a misaligned cause-effect argument. The implication is that young girls either don't know how they get pregnant (a patently ridiculous notion in this day and age) or don't know how to avoid it (also hard to imagine).

Now, your gut reaction is going to be to say something like: "Garbage!" "Nonsense!" or "That's ridiculous!" But comments like these are too strident for a group setting (although expressions of outrage often work well in a talk-show format—i.e., entertainment—which is a whole different forum).

All you have to do in a real-life group setting is to insert one word to make your point—"inappropriate." Then, phrase it as a question, not as a demand.

> **Comeback:** "You meant, *inappropriate* information about sex results in unwanted teen pregnancy, didn't you?"

Now the person who suggested that inadequate (or not enough) information on sex is the main problem has to debate *your* issue. You have instantly reframed the debate to your advantage.

Here are two more examples relating to misaligned arguments. Which is more accurate?

> ***a. Crime is caused by low self-esteem.***
>
> ***b. Low self-esteem contributes to delinquency.***

[*Think before continuing*.]

Answers: Both contain a kernel of truth. But the second statement is more accurate, because, looking only at Option A above, it is fair to ask *how many* delinquents have high self-esteem—too high, in fact. How about other reasonable causes of crime—idleness, lack of adult guidance and supervision, lack of religious/moral training, etc? The first statement (a), then —***"crime is caused by a low self-esteem"***—can either be debunked outright, or calls for some kind of qualification, such as: ***"Crime can be cause by low self-esteem."***

The second statement is okay because it already contains a qualifier: "*contributes to* delinquency." Yet, the statement is not a truism, because it is not true across the board. Nevertheless, you will find statement "b" used to bolster support for self-esteem programs. So, you might address the comment this way:

> **Comeback:** ***"Perhaps self-esteem is a factor in some children. But more likely causes are …."***

Then list some. With this retort, you've avoided a confrontation, but you have changed the focus of the debate. Instead of continuing to play up the merits of self-esteem, the person who made the original remark must now put more credible causes of delinquency on the table for discussion.

Another popular tactic of our opposition is the *appeal*—appeals to *fear*, to *expertise*, to *popularity*. Appeals are based on the power of suggestion, and that's why they work. Fortunately, most appeals are fairly easy to spot once you know what to look for, and you can nail your opponent on them.

An excellent example of the first, *appeal to fear*, is found in handout literature on climate change that characterizes detractors and critics as "deniers," "ultra-conservatives," and "fringe groups." The reader is to assume, of course, that nobody else ever complains. So the implied "fear" here is to be labeled a fanatic or zealot of some sort.

The *appeal to popularity* (a.k.a. "herd approval") is self-explanatory. Its roots are found in the inclination to conform and respond to the crowd.

When you hear the phrases "everyone knows," or "it's common knowledge that," or "we are all aware that," you have received a signal that an appeal to popularity and/or to fear are to follow. *Most people do not want to be the only person who "doesn't know" something or "isn't aware" of something*. We have a fear of seeming ignorant.

Feigning or citing *expertise* is another variation on the "appeal." Because of the aura surrounding the term "expert," it is easy to be misled. Behavioral and social "scientists" (typically psychologists and psychiatrists) for example, have been deified —by government, the courts, newspaper and magazine commentators, journalists, and countless others—to the point where their word is taken for gospel, not only in matters of mental health, but in education, for which they have little or no training. Nevertheless, you will frequently hear the lead-in phrase: "Most psychiatrists think…."

Openers like "most psychiatrists think…," and "most scientists say …," and are appeals to expertise. This does not mean that some psychiatrists or scientists don't say the things attributed to them. They may, and again they may not. *The problem is that, especially when facilitators use them, the appeal to supposed expertise is going to be used to justify, or build support for, whatever is coming next.* An audience has no way of knowing, without checking, whether "scientists believe that global warming over the last 100 years has caused the sea to rise one foot." In fact, many scientists contradict this claim.

Sometimes an expert in one field is suddenly cited as an expert in another, especially if s/he is well-known. Take the late Dr. Benjamin Spock, a well-known (if not always agreed-with) expert on pediatrics and general baby care in the 1950s and early 60s. Suddenly, during the Vietnam War, Spock became a spokesman for the anti-war faction. He was treated as an expert on foreign affairs, which was not his field.

Now, you can hold any views you like on the Vietnam War, but the point is that Dr. Spock's achievements in pediatrics did not qualify him as an authority on foreign affairs. When Hillary Clinton was named Secretary of State by President Barack Obama, critics pointed to the same problem: Mrs. Clinton's work as a lawyer and the fact of having once been a First Lady did not qualify her as an expert in foreign affairs.

The same goes for actress Jane Fonda, with her anti-war/anti-nuclear activism. Why should anyone care what she thinks in areas for which she has zero background? Who cares that Bruce Springsteen supported John Kerry, or that Bo Derek backed George W. Bush? These are appeals to popularity and imply an expertise which these celebrities do not possess. We caught a glimpse of the reality when actor-bodybuilder Arnold Schwarzenegger became Governor of California after ousting the former Governor in a special election with promises to get a handle on the budget. The budget in California wound up worse off than when Schwarzenegger took over. Why? One reason was lack of support among California's left-leaning media and legislators, but a greater reason was Schwarzenegger's unsuitability for the type of work he was so anxious to pursue, complex economics, despite his earnestness and his admirable refusal to take a salary for the job.

Another appeal is best reflected in the statements "everybody does it," and "he/she/they did it, too." These are called *appeals to common practice*.

Let's move now to the fallacy of ***Ill-Defined Terms***.

Global warming has been a perfect example here. Global warming actually started out as global cooling. We were going into a new ice age, according to studies publicized to great fanfare in the mid 1970s. When that didn't appear likely, wannabe socialists eager to redistribute the wealth and compromise American sovereignty came up with hogwash about carbon footprints—the same spokespersons who then proceeded to jet-set around the globe in private planes. Once global warming was exposed for the fraud it was, all the usual suspects changed terms again, this time to Climate Change.

People buy in to "junk science" because they do not know enough to contest it, and real scientists who could do so are "outed" and demonized before they can put up a decent counter-offensive. Those who don't play along are then and cut off from federal grants.

Again, **Sustainable Development (SD)** (see the Introduction to this manual) is a standout case in point. As indicated previously, SD is a positive-sounding phrase that is one part environmental extremism, one part economic statism, and one part social propaganda. All most people see is the environmental part of it, such as conservation, recycling and "energy-efficiency," and those are marketed in attractive packages with the help of an amenable media. If a credible person with scientific background could take the previous two sentences and boil them down to a well-articulated slogan-like definition, they might get just enough of a foot in the door that persons without such a professional background would be motivated to hear the rest of the story.

Instead, self-styled "experts" like Al Gore get to control the debate. He goes off on emotional tangents about polar bears (who are doing just fine, thank you) and whole cities under water (as if it had never happened before, and without any assistance from SUVs and electrical power plants).

Pro-lifers, on the other hand, pulled off a public relations coup when they redefined "fetus" as "the unborn." The word "fetus" had always carried the connotation of "a blob of tissue," until ultrasound technology began changing that perception. By applying the already-accepted term "*human* rights" to the unborn, pro-lifers probably saved hundreds of thousands of babies. True, there remain many willing to abort. But the fence-sitters were mostly swayed.

Section 8.- COUNTERING GROUP-THINK

In these final two scenarios—one long scenario, actually—you will learn how to avoid being trapped into group-think.

When you are in the room with other people, remember that so long as a facilitator is talking, you and the others cannot entirely concentrate on what you think or want to say. The facilitator will ask quest ions like:

What comes to your mind when I say sustainable development? "Urban sprawl"? "Greenhouse gases"?

The purpose of such questions is to get everyone comfortable, draw you out, and ***disrupt your train of thought by having to write things down.***

The facilitator also knows that you're probably thinking "me, and my concerns" and therefore unconsciously classifying everyone else as "not me." This is important because the facilitator is going to reorient you to think in terms of the group's ***stake*** in whatever is about to be presented. So, the facilitator moves the discussion toward an "us"—a stakeholder's—mentality.

In **Scenario 11** pretend you are in an open school board meeting facing the facilitator who works for Planned Parenthood of Chicago. The Chicago Board of Education already gave its approval in March 2001 to begin a $500,000 intensive sex-education ("intervention") program. But you don't know who this person really is. In the guise of moderator of this forum, the facilitator is actually a hired provocateur, here to sell you a graphic sex education program. S/he might start off by saying:

> **Facilitator:** *"Now, we don't want our youngsters to become AIDS statistics, do we? And we all know how devastating teen pregnancy can be."*

With this comment, s/he quickly pulls you into a group mentality by using the term "we." S/he wants you to focus on your stake in the big picture, not your own "selfish" principles.

That your neighbor's daughter may be raised quite differently from your own—allowed to watch raunchy movies at 11 and play obscene video games at 12—is of no concern to the facilitator. Both you and the mom next door are "in this crisis together." So, the facilitator lumps everyone together as "us."

As upstanding citizens, you would like to think, of course, that you and all the other parents in the group can rationally come to agree upon what is generally true for everyone. This is the facilitator's trump card—that all of you would like to think that you are rational beings who can work things out. While you are sitting there mulling over your concerns, everyone else in the room is doing the same. ***The task of the provocateur/facilitator is to turn everyone's individual concerns into "our concerns."***

You may not have come into the room with the least notion about your little Suzy engaging in sex relations at Saturday night's slumber party. You may not have given a thought to the kids at the school across town, like in Chicago's Clemente, Englewood and Harper school districts, with some 200 unwed pregnant teens and moms. (Day-care facilities were installed in 2001 inside some high schools there so that these young mothers would stay in school.)

As a facilitator, the provocateur will draw your attention to these things. Ever so covertly, s/he will ***control the environment of thought***. The provocateur doesn't give one hoot whether you think you have taught your daughter right from wrong, or that your child's family and church are doing more to preclude unmarried sexual relationships than anything the facilitator, the school, or the government can offer. S/he doesn't care that you may wish to preserve your child's innocence. The facilitator's lead-in line, therefore, will go something like this:

> **Facilitator:** *"You don't want Suzy to become AIDS statistics, do you?"*
>
> **You:** *"Frankly, I'm not worried about my daughter becoming an AIDS statistic."*

Let's stop right here. If I'm the facilitator, your response is helpful to me, not because I care about you or Suzy, but because now I know where you are coming from—just enough to decide how to handle you. *Too often, people are lulled into believing facilitators actually care about their views*. Given that this is not the case, **Facilitator** is going to ask a follow-up question:

> **Facilitator:** *"Oh? Why do you think you don't need to worry about your daughter becoming an AIDS statistic?"*
>
> **Parent:** *"Because I've taught my daughter right from wrong. I've taught her that sex is a sacred trust. I think sex should be equated with love, not with gross diseases."*

Again, great answer—if this was an honest discussion. But, you see, that was a self-serving question the facilitator just asked. S/he will use it against this parent later—to isolate her.

But first, the facilitator will probably quote statistics and drop the subject of your childrearing approach. Of course you have no way of checking them out at the moment. S/he may bring in five or six unwed teen mothers to tell their emotion-laden stories.

S/he will describe the effect of media influence on youthful sexual activity—*Desperate Housewives, Access Hollywood, Grey's Anatomy* and all the rest. Never mind that your family may not watch these programs. She will bring along a fist-full of sex-filled popular magazines like *Seventeen* and the teen version of *Cosmopolitan*.

You really can't argue with this stuff. So, the message becomes: Disaster! Crisis! We must do something!

All the group members will be confronted with the facilitator's version of "reality." Not with their concerns, but with "our concerns": media emphasis on sex, stalking predators, STD statistics, and more. Why, your Suzy might even end up being a White House intern for some lecher like Bill Clinton!! Who knows... So forget "your concern" that Suzy grow up to be a moral, modest, virtuous woman. Forget your preconceived notions about sex being sacred. The facilitator is going to try to win you all over to by casting you into an alternate reality.

So, let's go back to the "why do you think" question and take it from the top again, concentrating on what ***not*** to do:

> **Facilitator:** *"And just why don't you need to worry about your child becoming an AIDS statistic?"*
>
> **Parent 1:** *"I feel that way because I'm teaching my daughter to grow up to be a moral individual."*
>
> **Parent 2:** *"I feel that way because I think it's important to preserve childhood innocence instead of stealing it."*
>
> **Parent 3**: *"There are many parents here who feel that the*

> *subculture of teenage parenthood doesn't apply to us."*
>
> **Parent 4:** *"Most of us believe that sex is a private matter and not something that should be placed in front of the room like a billboard."*
>
> **Parent 5:** *"We feel it is inappropriate to compare our children to those brought up on the street."*
>
> **Parent 6:** *"I think the best way to avoid unwanted pregnancy and STDs is to teach abstinence."*

Question: Which parents gave answers that reflect good strategy? [*Think.*]

Answer: The ones who said "we feel" and "most of us" think.

Question: Why are these better answers?

Answer: Because they imply a united front, which will tend to scare off the facilitator.

Question: What about Parent 6. Did she deliver a whammy by mentioning abstinence?

Answer: Not in a strategic sense. Because now the facilitator is going to think, "Uh-oh!! I'd better launch a "brainstorming session."

The facilitator is going to get these guys into groups right away. Then *he* or *she* will deliver the whammy:

> **Facilitator**: *"Okay. Now, what are some alternatives to handling this problem in the way* (PARENT 6) *has suggested?"*

Question: Think about the facilitator's choice of words. What is s/he doing?

Answer: The facilitator is trying to ***control the environment of thought***. S/he hopes to get the group to "brainstorm" other solutions besides abstinence! The facilitator can't come right out and trash abstinence without giving away the game. Given the comments of Parents 1-6, s/he knows it won't do any good to argue with this group about abstinence. Instead, the facilitator has to work to involve everyone in alternative, group solutions.

Question: Why does the facilitator want to involve all members of the group in the solution? [*Think before continuing*.]

Answer: Because s/he wants to ensure that everyone feels the "solution" they come up with ***was their own idea, not the facilitator's***. But, of course, it will be the facilitator's idea, or more likely, the idea of Planned Parenthood, the Chicago Board, or whoever hired the facilitator and paid for the trip.

So, the Facilitator may ask various members of the group, starting with Melanie Jones, who hasn't said very much, and who might vacillate on this issue, judging from her earlier body language. Most group members will just assume the facilitator selected Mrs. Jones at random. *This will not be the case*. The fact is, the facilitator needs a break right now, and may think s/he knows how Melanie Jones will react. Most people don't make any attempt to hide their feelings, so the facilitator has made a mental note of every nod, smile, frown and raised eyebrow—and has a track record that is accurate enough to take a chance on Melanie Jones. Note how the facilitator phrases this question:

> **Facilitator:** *"What can we do, then, Melanie, besides (or in addition to) offering abstinence as a way to avoid unwanted pregnancy to our junior high school students?"*

> **Parent 7 (Melanie Jones):** *"Maybe we need more comprehensive sex-education programs."*

Eureka! Diversity reigns! The dialogue is now open. Because the facilitator got Mrs. Jones to bring up something besides abstinence, s/he may be able to manipulate the others into coming up with even more "progressive" options.

Question: How did the facilitator get away with not expanding upon the abstinence suggestion?

Answer: Because, by implication, that option was already on the table. Chances were good that no one would catch that. So, now the facilitator has two groups, pro and con, and s/he is going to encourage the "progressive" group. S/he will dump Parents 1-6 and flatter the other group members.

The "progressive" group will most likely offer such extremist ideas as: having teen mothers address grade-school children, showing films of male and female genitals infected with herpes and clap, mandating genital exams by school nurses, and displaying billboards for condoms in school hallways.

Parents 1-6, who wanted to preserve their children's innocence, are now gritting their teeth in fury. Everyone else is participating, going along with the "process." Their faction has suddenly become isolated. Why?

Answer: Because it is clear as a bell now, if it wasn't before, exactly which people don't care to discuss anything except abstinence. The psychological environment is now under the facilitator's control. Parents 1-6 are now in the position of setting aside their own concerns for the sake of moving forward, for the sake of the collective. Despite their qualms, they can at least try something new, right? They're not inflexible, right? They are being empowered to solve their own problems, right?

The subliminal message the facilitator is giving to Parents 1-6 is: Hey, adapt to life in the gray zone for the sake of society, or be ostracized.

Now, I'll quickly zoom in with the next step: See how the facilitator escalates the tension in **Scenario 12**. (But wait: **Facilitator** is in for a surprise!):

> **Facilitator:** *"You've all some done great brainstorming. Let's look at these ideas. Hmm… What about a pilot program through the psychology department at the university? We can bring in student volunteers who've actually had a sexually transmitted disease to discuss their experiences with our sixth-graders next month. Or, suppose we implement a pilot program with this new film demonstrating proper use of condoms in elementary schools for just 3 months? Just to see how it goes."*

Suddenly, [Melanie Jones raises her hand.]

> **Facilitator**: *"Yes, Melanie?"*
>
> **Melanie Jones:** *"You know, the only really effective means of reducing unwed pregnancy is to have monogamous sex within marriage. Maybe we ought to be discussing the abstinence education programs, too. How many abstinence programs have you brought for us to review?"*

WHOOPS! Mr. or Ms. Facilitator has miscalculated, has no answer, and now is revealed as biased.

Question: How did Melanie Jones pull this off?

Answer: By using a ***Principle of Psych-War***:

"Recruit persons who are highly intelligent but can appear to be stupid; who may seem to be dull but are in reality strong; who are vigorous and energetic, but can appear to weary easily; who are able to endure humiliation in order to succeed."

Mrs. Jones turned out to be a hero because she exposed the facilitator as a fraud and a plant.

Section 9 .- COGNITIVE DISSONANCE

There has been some confusion on the issue of cognitive dissonance since I discussed it in my books. It is another strategy used by the left to confuse opponents—but especially schoolchildren—and to establish group-think. Technically, the definition of cognitive dissonance is "a highly stressful mental or emotional reaction caused by trying to reconcile two opposing, inconsistent, or conflicting beliefs held simultaneously on any given subject."

The word cognition, as a stand-alone term, means "knowledge-based or factual." But the term cognitive has morphed into "that which is known or perceived; earnestly considered or pondered." Obviously, perceptions can be mistaken and therefore not necessarily factual. Nevertheless, when honest people refer to "cognitive curriculum" or "cognitive testing," they mean "substantive, factually based, or knowledge-based information." Dishonest educators, advertisers, and other expert manipulators view the word cognitive as "that which a person *perceives* as being true or factual." A huge difference!

Dissonant (dissonance), by itself, means "harsh, unpleasant, at variance, lacking harmony or agreement, incongruous." Obviously, this definition involves feelings and perceptions, as harshness and unpleasantness are emotional sensations. So, the two terms together—"cognitive dissonance"—translate to disorientation. That which you always thought to be true may not, in fact, be true, but you don't know how to sort it out. In fact, it is very uncomfortable to sort it out. Taken to extremes, this can wreak emotional havoc, lead to irrational behavior, and pull the rug out from under a person's belief system. That is to say, one's emotional life raft is in jeopardy.

When used by expert manipulators upon an unsuspecting populace—or worse, upon a "captive audience" (i.e., one that cannot get up and leave)—the purpose is to generate a mob mentality aimed at reversing previously accepted values. Thus, "truth" is turned against a person, just like many of our constitutional guarantees. Take "freedom of speech": This right has been turned against the very citizens it was originally designed to protect.

What makes "cognitive dissonance" so unethical in the hands of educators is that malleable and vulnerable young minds are serving as a political playground. The child is made uncomfortable to the point where he needs someone to reconcile the conflict which has raised his discomfort level. The educator, schooled for years in leftist rhetoric, must oblige. The child's parents, minister or rabbi usually come out the losers, while a whole new belief system composed of "new values" is inculcated. By the time the child is old enough to vote, join a union, or support a cause, the new values may well have taken hold and the traditional ones discarded or forgotten.

So, cognitive dissonance is a form of *mental coercion*. That is to say, it's not quite brainwashing and it's not quite subliminal advertising, either. It's more like setting a person up for a psychological fall. It plays with your mind by pitting not only various perceived "authorities" against each other, but by inducing discomfort using highly charged, sensitive topics. It works to shut down intellectual thought and heighten emotionalism.

To generate an "irreconcilable conflict," the manipulator must zero in on two opposing, but nevertheless firmly held, subconscious beliefs. In other words, the target subject doesn't know he's getting whacked because he may be unaware of his beliefs on a conscious level (especially the case with children), and he is certainly unprepared for his beliefs being challenged. The manipulator, however, has already pretty much figured out the unconscious beliefs of his subject through school surveys and assessments.

Take the 10-year-old pre-adolescent who assumes his parents are authority figures and trusts their judgment, even if he doesn't always like their rules. But his parents have also taught him that his teachers and school staff must be obeyed. There is nothing contradictory here. This is the way it is.

Enter the school counselor who says:

"You're a big boy now, Johnny. Your mom and dad are from another generation, you know, so it's not surprising they wouldn't be tolerant of gay people. You can make up your own mind. You wouldn't want a gay person to call you a 'dumb sports jock', now would you?"

In one fell swoop, the counselor has shaken Johnny's confidence and faith in his parents and, perhaps for the first time, made him question the merits of their teachings. Johnny is not really mature enough to understand just what gay people do, but judging from the counselor's comment, it's a sure bet that his parents oppose homosexuality. Johnny's curiosity about things sexual is still pretty much limited to differences in male and female private parts and anything concerning the bathroom.

Now let's examine exactly what the counselor has said. The counselor has whacked Johnny on five levels:

[1] Gives Johnny a justification for not abiding by his parents' values ("they're from another generation");

[2] Strokes Johnny's ego by telling him he is, in effect, more mature than he really is ("you're a big boy now");

[3] Plants the seed that his parents have major ethical problems ("it's not surprising they wouldn't be tolerant");

[4] Forces Johnny to choose between two opposing authorities under the pretext of thinking independently ("you can make up your own mind"); and, finally,

[5] Legitimizes a lifestyle choice his parents probably oppose ("you wouldn't want a gay person to call you a 'dumb sports jock', now would you?").

How can 10-year-old Johnny go to his parents with this? He can't. He probably won't even remember the context in which this conversation occurred. How can 10-year-old Johnny mull over this conflict? Well, he can't do that either, because the counselor has made it clear that a response is called for right now, on the spot. In fact, the counselor has offered to solve Johnny's discomfort by offering an immediate solution.

Johnny will probably be sullen and uncommunicative when he gets home, possibly without even remembering exactly the conversation with his counselor. His parents may be put off by this, interpreting it as "going through a phase." But the only "phase" many youngsters are going through, especially pre-adolescents, is the irreconcilable conflict established by an opposing authority, like the teacher or counselor.

Cognitive dissonance is dangerous in the hands of advertisers, too, especially those involved in generating campaigns for mass media consumption.

Managers create pop icons with little or no talent, dress them up like porn stars, and sell them to pre-adolescents as "artists." The danger posed by cognitive dissonance can be gauged by the level of harm induced. That harm is necessarily greater when the target is children rather than adults, who supposedly have the benefit of more experience and discernment.

While advertisements in general are marketing gimmicks aimed at getting us to do something, buy something, or change our views about something, not all rise to the definition of cognitive dissonance, even if they inflict some degree of harm. For example, an ad from the Humane Society that goes beyond helping unwanted animals to bolstering support against eating meat as "cruelty to animals" is not in the same category as the discussion with Johnny's school counselor. Why? *[Try to answer this question before moving ahead.]*

First, the Humane Society does not function as an authority figure, but merely as an advocacy group. Secondly, other than planting seeds of doubt, the ad fails to impact the audience on the five different levels Johnny encountered. Finally, and most significantly, the topic is debatable and does not require immediate action. So while the Humane Society may have stepped outside its usual function, it has only offered a new topic for discussion.

Some ads, however, *do* induce cognitive dissonance in those pre-disposed to a highly repetitive message. For example, most ads aimed at teenage girls show bodies that are thin to the point of looking sickly, instead of the rounded feminine figures the over-55 crowd grew up with. This message, repeated in magazines, film, billboards, and television leads many girls to starve themselves or eat only low-fat and non-fat foods (which have been determined as hard to digest, especially in developing teens and the elderly, and to have high calorie counts despite their lesser fat content). This trend has resulted in behaviors previously unheard of (bulimia, anorexia, obsessive "fitness" regimes, etc.). Taken separately, these ads are not examples of cognitive dissonance. But together, they induce a skewed view of what is healthy and beautiful, driving youngsters once again to compulsive actions without having given the matter thought.

The following is an example of cognitive dissonance established as part of a classroom activity or lesson:

In an Allegheny County, Pennsylvania, middle school science class, a "science" film opened with an idyllic, rustic landscape—birds singing in the trees, mother ducks leading their young on a pleasant excursion down a creek, rabbits scampering over the ground. The scene oozed fresh air and sunshine.

Suddenly an immense tractor-bulldozer appeared. The camera zoomed in on the word "AMERICAN" emblazoned on the side of the yellow vehicle. This designation was actually the name of the company that made the equipment, but young children would interpret it only as "an American bulldozer."

Due to the camera angle, the vehicle looked much like a tank, very imposing, and it was overturning everything in its path. Shrubs and grass were torn apart. Exhaust filled the air.

A man jumped out of the front seat and went over to the embankment to drain the creek where the ducklings had been following their mother. Another man brought over a can of gasoline, poured it over portions of the surrounding area and ignited it. As the pair drove away, flames leapt into the air. Trees caught fire. Living creatures ran for cover.

Suddenly the ducklings, which by that time had emerged onto the other side of the creek, were overcome by encroaching flames and burned alive. Nests of baby birds came crashing to the ground, and the camera zoomed in on what was left. In a final close-up, the tractor-bulldozer was shown plowing under the remains of the nest, the ducklings, and some bird eggs.

As the scene receded from the screen, this sentence flashed: "Man cannot foresee or forestall. He will end by destroying the earth."

This film, "The Cry of the Marsh," was shown in the early 1980s. So, there was no "morphing" technology involved in making the film. What you saw was whatever they had to do to get the whole business on film. After the film, the students were divided into groups for a follow-up activity, "Who Shall Populate the Planet?"

This film meets the definition of cognitive dissonance. Why? *[Try to answer before continuing.]*

First of all, there is the issue of subliminal deception and psychological impact: the way "AMERICAN" was depicted, camera angle, shock value of the carnage. Because of these things, there was no issue to debate. The film aimed for the gut, not for intellectual discussion. For all the kids knew, the men in the film were creating this mayhem for pleasure, not to construct or create anything. There is no mention that forests occasionally are deliberately burned to avoid a more disastrous fire later on from natural causes, such as lightening strikes.

Finally, the follow-up exercise demands an immediate decision—made by consensus, of course, and under pressure—based on what the young viewers had seen. By the time the kids get home, they will probably have forgotten the relationship of the follow-up exercise to the film and, therefore, will have no context to bring to their bewildered parents, who will hear comments like: "You don't care if you're destroying the Earth!" Parents aren't likely to see either the film or the follow-up exercise. Both will be long gone by the time parents approach school officials.

Cognitive dissonance is used against the child in the classroom, in songs, video games and ads aimed at kids. It affects adults, too—in meetings, on committees and in focus groups. The tactic relies to a large extent on muddying the concept of "authority." With children, various authority figures are played against each other. The parent, for example, is the child's first and most natural authority figure. But the parent also tells the child that his teacher is an authority figure, not perhaps in so many words, but by transmitting the idea that this person has to be respected and obeyed. The policeman is an authority figure, as are the family's minister or rabbi.

What happens, then, when one of these authority figures forces the child to choose between them or to marginalize one of them? The answer will largely depend on which authority figure the child spends the most time with and which one the child perceives as the greater threat to his feelings or well-being.

Thanks to a culture that increasingly keeps children with their peers and away from their parents, most youngsters today actually view their peers as the authority figures—and as the persons having the greatest affect on their well-being. Unethical educators and school counselors capitalize on this; they actually use children to punish and report on other children and then call it "peer pressure." What it really is, is psychological warfare using children as human shields against each other.

Why do this? Educators want each child to stop thinking independently and default to a defensive, group (consensus) mentality. If the group accepts homosexual behavior as "normal," for example, then any child who doesn't becomes "an outsider." He's being set up to forego personal integrity in favor of feeling accepted, *to "need" his peers more than he needs his principles*.

Now think about this, because some readers may be too young to recall, but there was a time when children didn't necessarily want to be one of the crowd. Most actually preferred to stand out and be noticed. But this mentality has been discouraged for a long time. The herd must think alike, except in competitive sports, and even then, one never hears enough about "the team effort."

Let's take an example from sports (a form of entertainment) to show how "standing out" as a performer does not when it comes to ideas. Recall Olympic champion ice skater Katerina Witt, who posed nude a few years ago for *Playboy* magazine. Now, Ms. Witt has always been daring and that was her choice. More interesting, however, were subsequent interviews with her skating colleagues. When asked their thoughts on Ms. Witt posing for girlie pictures, the interviewees used words like "brave," "confident" and "sophisticated" to describe her actions. None suggested the photos indicated, perhaps, a lack of self-confidence, inasmuch as Ms. Witt was past the age of 30; or that this type of publicity demeaned the person and the sport. If any interviewees thought these things privately, it would never find its way into mainstream print or on the air.

If a child under the old Soviet regime had told his teacher he thought private property and free markets were great ideas, he would have been sent to a re-education center, his parents denied their pension, and many career slots would be closed to him until he proved he was "cured" of his heresy against the state. The difference in America is that nobody will get shot, moved to a gulag or automatically have his pension suspended. But he will be ostracized and ridiculed, a little note (such as "homophobic") may appear in his electronic portfolio/dossier, and he may never know whether that promotion he didn't get was caused by something he said having marked him as "inflexible," "intolerant" or "dogmatic."

For example, on December 5, 2002, Senate Majority Leader Trent Lott (R-Miss.) attended former Senator Strom Thurmond's (D-S.C.) 100th birthday party. Thurmond became a Republican in 1964, but in 1948 ran for President as a "Dixiecrat" on a states' rights platform—something politically incorrect since the 1990s all by itself. Everyone, of course, was trying to say nice things at the party about the elderly Senator who, in fact, died the next year. So, Trent Lott—with strategic cluelessness so typical of conservative politicians, spouted that "When Strom Thurmond ran for president, we voted for him. We're proud of it. And if the rest of the country had followed our lead, we wouldn't have had all these problems over the years, either."

Unfortunately, Thurmond had opposed the Civil Rights Movement and later, the 1964 Civil Rights Act with the allegation that the Act illegally overturned the Separation of Powers under the United States Constitution. Regardless of his true motives (he was born in 1902, after all), he may have been technically correct concerning the Separation of Powers, which Congress and the Executive Branch have been violating with impunity for all kinds of reasons ever since).

The upshot for Trent Lott, though, having been heard loudly and clearly by reporters, who printed his remark, was that he was pressured to give up his position as Senate Majority leader based on make-nice well-wishing at an old man's birthday party. Maybe he was referring to other stances by Strom Thurmond, maybe not. (This would not have happened to a liberal or leftist Democrat, of course, although National Public Radio's firing of liberal commentator Juan Williams came close, for his passing remark in a 2010 interview that he gets nervous seeing person in Moslem headdress boarding a flight he is on.) Thus, crimes of opinion have come a long way toward ensuring the marginalization of individuals.

There are other downsides to the practice. For one thing, if you say something, you tend to be stuck with it. That means you do not have the luxury of being allowed to change your mind—something at least one Founder of our nation, Thomas Paine, disputed in his tome, *Common Sense*. The issue hits home today: For example, if you believed abortion was okay in 1975, and then changed positions in the year 2000, that marks you as a hypocrite and flip-flopper. If a legislator agreed that a Transportation Security Administration was needed to thwart hijackings in the late 1980s, but then decided in the year 2010 that the civil rights abuses outweighed the benefits, particularly when the Department of Homeland Security sprung a surprise groping policy on boarding passengers during the Thanksgiving rush, the legislator's prior approval will be trotted out by government to bolster its decision. If you ran for school board on a platform of increased security in the wake of the 1999 Columbine shooting, but then reversed position when school officials started demanding that innocent young honor students remove their underpants in front of school staff in a ridiculous and humiliating search for simple ibuprofen (as per the 2009 case of Arizona teen, Savannah Redding, at Safford Middle School, which she won in court), well, you are stuck with your former position again, and must hold nothing less than a formal press conference to reverse your viewpoint. Even worse outcomes await young test-takers down the road when whatever opinion they checked off on a standardized school test follows them in college and on into the workplace via Longitudinal Studies.

As a parent, you are going to have to explain to your child how the group can be used by expert manipulators to force-feed certain values and worldviews, or at least get youngsters to write down somewhere what they think their superiors want to see.

This means advising the child concerning the limits of a teacher's "authority." For sure, you need to tell your child that television commentators and movie stars are neither authority figures nor, for the most part, experts on any subject. You must emphasize the importance of independent thinking while at the same time explaining, like parents did in the old Soviet Union, the potential drawbacks of saying what one really thinks. In other words, we *don't* have free speech or free conscience right now, and it is necessary to pick one's battles carefully.

At the same time, you must safeguard yourself against cognitive dissonance, especially in forums where citizen groups are brought together under the guise of making decisions, forming policy, or lending support to some initiative that has, in fact, already been determined. If your family doesn't practice recognizing and countering cognitive dissonance, neither you nor your children will have any chance of maintaining control over personal values and opinions, much less be able to persuade others to your beliefs. Among the most important information you can get—ahead of meeting time, if possible—includes: Who is serving as the facilitator, speaker, host, or sponsor? Who pays the bills? Who signs the checks?

In addition, whenever a hot-button topic is on a meeting's agenda, it is critical to know the following:

- Who, or what organization/agency, is sponsoring, funding, and/or promoting the program or concept in question.
- Where the organization/agency gets its funding.

- Who heads the organization/agency and their credentials.
- Who stands to benefit financially from the program or idea.

And **never** take ***"none"*** or ***"no one"*** for an answer.

Summary: Principles of Verbal Combat

I. Know when you are under attack.

- If you cannot spot verbal aggression, you will be a perfect target.
- Do not assume you are "oversensitive," "paranoid," "reactionary," "narrow," or that you "just don't get it." If something doesn't sound right, there is probably a reason.

II. Know what kind of attack is being employed.

- Learn to identify the basic structures of fallacious reasoning.
- Learn to gauge the skill of your adversary and other participants.

III. Make your defense appropriate to the attack.

- Remember that a stock response is not always the right one to use.
- Frequently the best defense is a good offense.

IV. When targeted, always question the opponent's assumption(s) instead of taking the bait.

V. Follow through and play to win.

- Do not feel guilty about fighting back.
- This appears to be more difficult for women than for men. (More husbands and fathers need to get into the fray instead of leaving it all to the women.)

Two self-tests can be found at the end of this manual, a Mid-Test and a Final Exam. TAKE THE "MID-TEST" now. Save the Special Exam on Education Issues for <u>after</u> the Advanced Course, as this test leans heavily on the book, ***Cloning of the American Mind**: Eradicating Morality through Education,* also by Beverly Eakman. Answer Keys follow the two tests, along with a grading scale.

ADVANCED COURSE:
Hard-Ball Attack Strategies

GENERAL INTRODUCTION

Your adversaries are always on the offense and never work from a defensive position—one secret of their success. For example, several "attack publications" have come out in recent years to help school staff and leftist lobbying organizations rebuff increasing criticism of our nation's schools. Among the more prolific sources of pamphlets, manuals, booklets and workshops aimed at deflecting criticism and stereotyping detractors are the National Education Association (NEA), its state chapters and spin-offs, like the Association for Supervision and Curriculum Development (ASCD). Other sources include the Education Commission of the States (ECS); the American Civil Liberties Union (ACLU); and People for the American Way (PAW), and a smaller, alternate teachers' union, the American Federation of Teachers (AFT).

Such organizations are financially secure. Many receive grants from left-leaning foundations such as the Carnegie, Ford, Johnson, and Rockefeller Foundations or the Aspen Institute for Humanistic Studies. They may work through universities (which benefit from state and federal grant monies). They launch curriculums and general initiatives to indoctrinate upcoming educators and the general public into an anti-parent, pro-socialist mindset. They seek to prepare teachers entering the profession to expect "nutty" parents who criticize policies, programs, and curriculums.

These organizations appeal to young teachers' already inflated egos by portraying them as "experts" and characterizing parents as bumbling amateurs, regardless of any expertise a parent might possess in his or her own field. The success of this tactic may seem puzzling, since many teachers and legislators are themselves parents. But such is the result of indoctrination. Educator-parents, for example, don't see it that way, thanks to some 40 years of "programming" long before they hit college. They see themselves as enlightened and everyone else as part of the "unwashed masses."

So, the fact that a large percentage of teachers and Washington politicians send their own children to private schools does not strike educators as hypocritical; they see it as removing their own youngsters from the "unwashed masses." So the first thing you have to realize is that most educators believe they are part of an exclusive elite. Their union, such as the NEA (or for federal employees, a fast-growing union, the American Federation of Government Employees (AFGE), an outgrowth of the well-known AFL-CIO) appeals to the overblown sense of importance and status so typical of government bureaucracies.

The NEA, for example, claims it is "empowering" teachers. Never mind that in 2001, their education majors scored 20 out of 23 compared to all majors in both the verbal and math portions of the SATs.

School administrators get a more hard-hitting version of the same elitist indoctrination. They view teachers as "the hired help" with a responsibility to make principals and superintendents look good in the media. This "responsibility" does not extend to ensuring young pupils leave school with factual knowledge. It means appeasing and entertaining kids so they will stay in school and be reasonably compliant while they are there. It means bolstering test scores by any means necessary, including teaching the test or inflating grades, to bolster public relation showing smiley-faced kids.

Both factions, teachers and administrators, have bought into the view that attitudes and opinions supersede knowledge; that facts constantly change; and that it is better to create students who are flexible, tolerant, and amenable to "change" than it is to turn out youngsters who can think outside the box and provide them with substantive information. Thus do administrators and teachers scratch each other's backs on the issue of grades, while at the same time maintaining a strained and generally hostile relationship to the casual observer. Teachers complain they don't get any backup from their administrators (true); administrators complain teachers are incompetent (also largely true).

What you as a parent and taxpayer need to understand is that most such combative relationships have been carefully engineered by skilled tacticians, such as those in the colleges and universities, which have been at it since the 1960s. Tacticians have lobbyists, and at lest in this context, all have a vested interest in the *political*, not the intellectual, outcome.

By the time the universities get through with graduating educators, be they teachers or administrators, a built-in bias and hostility has already been inculcated toward parents as well as toward traditional principles in general. Graduates who are truly conscientious and open-minded face an uphill battle; once "discovered" by their higher-ups; for example, such teachers get the worst classes and the least support in the hope they will leave or retire early.

There are numerous examples of "attack literature" and left-leaning training texts which have surfaced in recent years. Among the most vicious early versions is a 1976 text, *Training for Change Agents* by Ronald and Mary Havelock. It carries such sections as "Extinguishing Existing Attitudes, and Behaviors in a Person" (p. 44 of that text). Examining closely, one will find the imprint on the cover, barely visible, "ISR," which Institute for social Research, a Moscow-based institution specializing in propaganda. The reference section reads like a "Who's Who" of behavioral Centers and experts. The cherry-on-the-sundae is a contact number from the U.S. Office of Education under the old Department of Health, Education and Welfare, which provided the contract and accompanying funding to pen and disseminate the text.

Then there's the 1975 contract between Rand Corporation and the same U.S. Office of Education to write a series of six so-called Change Agent Projects entitled "Federal Programs Supporting Educational Change." Volume II gives a not-so-subtle hint as to what's inside: "Factors Affecting Change Agent Projects." In other words, professional provocateurs and agitators spearheaded "changes" which by the 1990s had thoroughly infected K-12 institutions—and not for the better. The thrust of both the Havelock text and the Rand series is attitudinal, pushing substantive learning to the back burner.

Organizing Social Change: A Manual for Activists in the 1990s, put out in 1991 by Seven Locks Press (whose headquarters originated in Washington, D.C., prior to setting up shop three other major metropolises), is at least more honest in its choice of title. The Index comes complete with the lyrics for some 13 protest songs, including one aimed at ***universal health care***, which in 2010 became Obamacare. You get the picture.

For the sake of brevity, then, we will take up three examples of "attack literature" to demonstrate, first, the utter viciousness of your opposition and, second, to examine potential counter-attacks to stem the worst abuses. Remember the remainder of the manual you are studying is aimed at individuals seeking office, conservative lobbyists and other activists who have already successfully mastered Part I. Now, we will work with three publications:

a) "The Attack by the U.S. Religious Right on 'Government Schools' or 'Who was that masked man who stole our education reform?", by Richard P. Manatt with Guest Writer Joe Drips, International Journal of Education Reform, September/October 1993 (pre-publication copy), used as required reading for education administration course (Ed. Ad. 541) at Iowa State University, Ames, Iowa, hereafter referred to as the Manatt/Drips pamphlet ;

b) "What's Left After the Right? A Resource Guide for Educators," by Janet L. Jones, Ed.D., for the Washington Education Association, a state chapter of (and funded by) the National Education Association, 1986, (195 pages), hereafter referred to in abbreviated form as the NEA manual ; and

c) "How to Deal With Community Criticism of School Change," a publication of the NEA spin-off organization, the Association for Supervision and Curriculum Development (ASCD) and the Carnegie Foundation spin-off, the Education Commission of the States (ECS), 1993, hereafter referred to as the ASCD/ECS handbook.

Section 10.- "ATTACK" PUBLICATIONS AND REBUTTALS

Attack publications are noteworthy not only for what they state, but for what they omit; for their use of "black PR" (smears), and for distortions of fact. They also help us—occasionally, when they reflect what their writers honestly believe—to comprehend our opponents' prejudices, which then can be used to our advantage.

For example, in a glossary of terms found in the Manatt/Drips pamphlet, it states that the Religious Right (which includes everybody who takes exception to a school policy, curriculum, text, program, or activity) opposes "global education" (renamed "multicultural studies") on the grounds that it promotes vegetarianism and tells children that their country isn't the best. The prospective school administrators who studied this text as part of their preparatory course work were told that the real definition of global education was "the study of cultures, economics, languages, governments, and ecosystems, worldwide." However, there were no materials to back up this claim—no references to the tomes of revered globalists like James Becker, who stated, among other things, that man was "the most destructive of all animals"; to John Goodlad's *Schooling for a Global Age*; or to Benjamin Bloom's *Taxonomy of Educational Objectives*, in which he asserted that education was primarily about "challenging children's fixed beliefs." Thus, either the course's creators really didn't know what the criticisms of global education were, or they knew but didn't care to present the facts, preferring instead to create a negative reaction toward *any* critic of global (a.k.a. "multicultural") education, whose aim is to water down national sovereignty in the mode of what is now called **"Sustainable Development (SD)**," which in turn is based on something called ***Agenda 21*** (the "21" referring to the year 2021, by which time a complete transformation of American society is supposed to have taken place).

Nearly all attack publications aimed at helping communities and schools deflect criticism contain descriptive passages associating "critics" with organizations, political persuasions, and theological perspectives they think will turn people off. In general, critics are characterized as "extremists" who seek to misinform the general public or advance a narrow agenda. Critics of education are categorized as out-of-touch individuals who believe that "all we have to do is to go back to the way we did things in the 1950": in other words, "reactionaries," a smear.

Other blanket smears used to describe critics include:

- Religious Right
- Far-Right
- Right-Wing
- Radical Right (replaces "New Right" and "Moral Majority")
- Conservative and/or Ultra-Conservative
- Christian and/or Christian Fundamentalists
- Censors
- Lunatic Fringe

None of these categories may apply to the person criticized, especially scientists at odds with SD or Agenda 21.

Nevertheless, attack publications end up labeling all critics "enemies of education," which translates to "enemies of the State," and constitutes, therefore, of course is a blatant oversimplification (see Section 6) you can nail them on. Accusations run the gamut from exaggerated to highly biased and totally false.

For the most part, the manuals' writers above base their smears on the writings and presentations of the most strident and least articulate critics, using these individuals as catch-all stereotypes. Well-spoken and highly respected critics, including even those from their own camp (e.g., Juan Williams of National Public Radio in 2010), eventually are cast into the extremist mold. Only rarely are criticisms rebutted point by point.

If you are handed one of these attack publications—it may be just a flyer—it is best to handle it as a straw-man argument (review Section 6):

> **Comeback:** ***"You know, I haven't actually seen what this person wrote or heard him speak. Before I decide, I'd like to see more."***

Like most of us, readers of attack manuals—which are aggressively distributed to prospective and in-service teachers and administrators, school board members, community and business leaders, selected religious leaders, and even politicians —are not well enough versed in the tricks of the rhetorical trade to pick up on the subtleties of implied stereotyping and labeling.

As per the Manatt/Drips pamphlet, individual critics of educational programs, policies, or curriculums are characterized as ***"good, salt of the earth, concerned parents and/or community***

members"; but absolutists in their beliefs, which is a no-no. Usually they are cast as ***"ultra-conservatives, fundamentalists, evangelicals"*** or just someone who has ties to "Far Right" organizations; along with people who are ***"willing to devote days, weeks, months and years to their cause"*** (as if our adversaries are not).

Some of the more highly criticized opponents of political correctness are misidentified as "Christian"—especially teachers in the "look-say," or "whole language," reading camp; global-warming "skeptics" and psychological testing opponents. By identifying phonics and skeptical scientists or doctors with Christians, as per the NEA manual, the method is immediately marginalized in the minds of those already been "prepped" to view anything "Christian" as suspect.

Stereotyping may be based on an *appeal to fear* (see Section 6). The purpose is not only to de-legitimize specific criticisms and to censor critics, but to scare so-called mainstream organizations, such as the Republican Party; the Presbyterian Church USA; conservative news outlets' and high-profile independent columnists, politicians and researchers into "backing off" for fear of losing face and being marginalized along with those already on the hit list. Thus, many well-known public figures will go only so far in their criticism. This explains the reticence of commentators for FOX news and others to being outspoken critics of the homosexual agenda, regardless of their private opinions. After all, they have bills to pay—college tuitions and mortgages—just like everybody else. While their hearts may be in the right place, marginalization may be too high a price to pay for outrage.

In *CLONING OF THE AMERICAN MIND*, I provide a lengthy listing of those groups, columnists, publications and politicos most frequently characterized as "enemies" of education (or the State) in attack manuals, flyers, and handbooks. These groups often are falsely linked by our adversaries to neo-Nazi groups like the Ku Klux Klan.

So, be very wary of group-linking unless you can prove it. Forget whether you *approve* of the group to which a person or organization is being linked or likened. *The real question is: Are they truly linked?* If so, how? Did a couple of members of both groups just happen to attend the same college? Did one organization purchase materials from the other? If the "link" is based only on such loose, circumstantial evidence, it's not good enough.

Note that many blackballed entities do not equally share all political beliefs across-the-board. Unfortunately, if they share even *one* belief with any of the others on the list, they will be categorized. Therefore, the continual "I am not!" game that some of us play is a losing battle.

Unlike our side, our adversaries don't care who their members work with or what they stand for as long as each can be counted on to contribute significantly to some particular issue on the agenda. The left, however, knows that we are more particular about whom *we* work with, and they never fail to capitalize on that. We need to reconsider our strategy.

Who Does Our Opposition Think They Are?

In general, our "working opposition" portrays itself as the "voice of reason." As per the NEA manual, they see themselves as:

> ***"[p]ersons with a . . . moderate perspective [who] believe that public education is an essential societal entity through which children of all ethnic groups and religious (or non-religious) persuasions, learn to think creatively, productively and critically . . . [and] who promote a diverse curriculum that provides children with the mental tools by which they may survive and compete in a highly technical and rapidly changing world."***

This comes across as sensible, upbeat, and progressive. Most significantly, perhaps, our "working opposition" sees itself as "committed to excellence…educat[ing] the whole person to be a caring involved citizen of a global society." This applies equally to schoolchildren and to the reader of the newspaper (the left is so well-funded that they can afford to give away abridged copies of their newspapers at subway stops, office buildings, etc.

First and foremost among our immediate opponents—that is, the ones most likely to involve us in a direct confrontation and craft attack manuals (the "big guns")—are the ones who call themselves "Friends of Education." They may even happily characterize themselves as "liberals," but never as leftists,

Marxists or as cooperating eugenics and psychological drug-proponent organizations. A partial list includes:

- People for the American Way
- The National Education Association and its state and local affiliates
- The Council of Chief State School Officers
- The Education Commission of the States
- The American Civil Liberties Union
- Americans for Separation of Church and State
- Americans for Religious Liberty
- The National Coalition Against Censorship
- The Carnegie Foundation for the Advancement of Teachers (and its spin-offs)
- The Rockefeller Foundation
- The Danforth Foundation
- The Ford Foundation
- The Aspen Institute for Humanistic Studies
- The Kettering Foundation
- The Robert Wood Johnson Foundation
- The Association for Supervision and Curriculum Development
- The National Council for Social Studies
- The American Library Association
- The American Association of School Administrators
- The Freedom to Read Foundation
- The National School Boards Association
- The World Population Council
- The American Eugenics Society (renamed Society for the Study of Social Biology, 1972)

- New York Coalition for Democracy
- Coalition for Choice
- The Humanist Society (British and U.S.)
- The Lambda and Empire State Pride Agenda
- Planned Parenthood and SIECUS (Sex Information and Education Council if the U.S.)
- behaviorist colleges like Esalen Institute
- National Women's Political Caucus (militant feminists)
- AFL-CIO (not in every state)
- Bill and Melinda Gates Foundation (huge U.N. contributors)

A note of caution: It is important to recognize that not all of our adversaries, including some on this list, are "co-conspirators." Some have been drawn into the Illiteracy Cartel—either because they truly believe a few of the erroneous stands spouted by the real conspirators (like the Carnegie Foundation and the Aspen Institute) and/or because they are not as well-educated on the specifics as they think. For example, some of the entities on the list couldn't tell you the anything about the background or works of John Dewey, his alliances or supporters. They couldn't explain the philosophy of Benjamin Bloom, Ralph Tyler, or the Carnegie Foundation, much less the contributions of key Marxists like Antonio Gramsci or Herbert Marcuse (examined in my book *CLONING OF THE AMERICAN MIND*).

Most people today, unfortunately, have no incentive or desire to learn about the roots of their so-called beliefs. One could argue that a psychologically controlled environment is frequently constructed by default.

The point is that the opponents you are likely to encounter in meetings, forums, panels and committees won't necessarily be "the big guns." They may, however, have been trained by the "big guns." If an issue reaches a boiling point, or is expected to cause a furor, "the big guns" are often called upon for funds and "technical support," which is why, in running for public office either locally or at the state and federal level, every poll may indicate you are winning; then you find you suddenly are losing.

Where Do The "Big Guns" Get Their Clout?

Our nation is a rich land, and much of that wealth is concentrated in the so-called nongovernmental organizations, or NGOs. The list is endless. They range from trusts and endowments for research, many totally obscure, to centers for policy studies, popularly called "think-tanks." Groups promoting or trying to stop this or that; councils for the advancement-of-whatever; and a mind-boggling array of foundations, a few of which, like Carnegie and Rockefeller, tend to call the shots in conservative think-tanks. What they do is give just enough money to have a say in what goes on. Conservatives, never flush with funds anyway, take the bait—and seal their fate.

Some NGOs are dedicated to research, some to discussion or to charity; others are devoted to single-issue propaganda, lobbying, publicity, enhancement of public awareness, or some combination of these, depending upon what kind of tax structure they want (or think they can get away with).

When NGOs join forces, they can accomplish a lot. Consider an October 16, 1997, Associated Press (AP) report stating that 22 big corporations had joined with 16 foundations to fight "a national crisis in the quality of early childhood programs"—an announcement timed to coincide with the Clinton White House's Child Care Conference the following week. It was scripted to bolster the mental health industry's push to get kids away from their parents and into "quality" day care, despite the insistence of many professionals, including some psychologists, who said that it is too much child care, as opposed to not enough, that was doing the harm. Nevertheless, the AP announcement sounded good to the uninformed. Among the foundations jumping on the bandwagon were, of course, the Carnegie Corporation, the Rockefeller Brothers Fund, and the Ford Foundation. Our side, meanwhile, rarely is organized enough to achieve this kind of cooperation.

Did the initiative provide any long-term gains for society? No. They practically never do.

As world-renown novelist Frederick Forsyth has noted, the Nation's Capital is the headquarters for some 1,200 NGOs: New York alone has around 1,000. All have "deep pockets." Many, or most, are tax-exempt, especially those set up by a long-deceased philanthropist. Some get tax dollars via government grants. Others, like the Gates Foundation and the Robert Wood Johnson Foundation (RWJ), are spinoffs of private industry—in this case, the Microsoft empire and Johnson & Johnson, respectively. RWJ is responsible for many controversial mental health programs and graphic sex-education initiatives in the schools.

In his novel *Icon,* Forsyth writes that NGOs are the "nesting places for academics, politicians, former ambassadors, do-gooders, busy-bodies and even the occasional maniac." In a republic like ours, power equals influence. Only under a dictatorship does raw power exist within the law. Thus, the implication in recent history and civics texts that America is a "democracy," period, not a "republic."

Unelected power in a democracy lies in the ability to to mobilize public opinion through slick marketing, lobbying, and that most sophisticated form of bribery known as the charitable "donation" or "contribution" from which some sort of recompense is expected—a situation on the rise in the U.S. If an NGO becomes powerful enough, its influence may require no more than what is known as "the quiet word"—a piece of well-placed advice to an office-holder or policymaker.

Snoop Surveys

Many attack manuals make use of the "snoop survey." For example, the *Wall Street Journal* published on its editorial page one such survey, mailed to New York State Superintendents in April 1997 by the New York Coalition for Democracy (a liberal, mental "health" advocacy group).

The survey in question listed 29 "ultra-Right" organizations and asked survey recipients whether they were aware of any materials or literature emanating from these sources. Specific information was also requested concerning how the recipient became aware of "conservative" materials. Possibilities included supermarket flyers, voters' guides, letters to the schools, and letters-to-the-editor in local papers. Readers were asked to note red-flag terms like "family values" and "dumbing down."

The survey went on to ask whether there had been any known attempts to "censor, remove, or relocate," especially in a religious or sexual context, materials from school libraries. Questions followed regarding any letter-writing campaigns, protests, or anti-funding threats by conservative groups relating to school speakers, plays, the arts, programs, or exhibits.

Then, the capital offense: *"Are there any faith-based churches [which] have endorsed school-board candidates or questioned the Constitutional separation of church and state in your District? Please be specific."*

This goes a step beyond the usual. By using the term "faith-based," rather than the typical smear—"fundamentalist" or "Christian Right"—left-wing writers went right for the jugular. "Faith-based religion" is revealed as the true pariah. Thus did faith-bashing become more pronounced post-9/11.

The **"snoop survey"** is a typical tactic, and unfortunately, most of the groups on *our* side are either unable or unwilling to accumulate any tidbits concerning the activities of our adversaries. Too many activists leading the charge for academic excellence, for example, are forever preaching to the choir. Same for critics of environmental extremism. We mail out opinion-style surveys to *loyalists* filled with questions skewed to obtain a predictable response, usually for fund-solicitation purposes. But this doesn't influence anyone *new*, and it irritates those who give frequently so that they stop giving to avoid another solicitation.

Sowing Seeds

The NEA manual is a hefty 195 pages long—longer than most how-to's of its kind. Like most, however, its stated purpose is "to assist school personnel who have experienced, are experiencing or who project they will experience the conflict and trauma of a censorship controversy." This tactic is an appeal to fear (see Section 6).

The key words in the above quotation are "project they will experience" and "trauma." The implication is that all schools can expect to be approached by a bunch of nuts who will throw an entire school or school system into turmoil. A sense of urgency is imparted.

Several states have modified the **NEA manual** for their own use, such as the State of Washington. In typical fashion, Washington's manual begins with a list of interchangeable terms (smears) used to describe the enemies of education, called "censors": Ultra-Right, Far Right, etc. This is followed by a **"Background and Update on Censors vs. Public Education."**

The subtitle above is reminiscent of what we learned in the Beginner-Intermediate phases of this manual. What methodology (besides a smear) is employed in the above subtitle? **[*Think before continuing.*]**

Answer: Framing the debate. Your opposition, in this case the writer of the manual, has just framed the debate—planted the idea that it is not merely "opponents" whom school personnel will be dealing with, but fanatics. Moreover, when you show up to protest curriculum on phony global warming at the school or in some other forum, there will already be one strike against you, whether anybody says so or not—the label "fanatic." This is sure to put many other participants on the defensive right away—a position you may find difficult to overcome. The deck is stacked against you.

But not everyone will be reached by your opponents; not everyone will "buy in." *Your task is to reframe the debate and "plant seeds" of your own.* So, as they say in baseball: "Keep your eye on the ball" (the goal), not on the unfairness of your opponents.

It's easier to keep a cool head if you focus on the technicalities of a question or issue instead of reacting to emotional "bait." Focus on the method, not the emotive language. Ask yourself repeatedly: What is my opponent using against me? Eventually you will have to teach your children to do this too, or they will never be able to hold onto their values and opinions at the college level.

The **NEA manual** admonishes readers that anything that is "outside the realm of the beliefs of the...Religious Right is considered anti-Christian, unpatriotic, demeaning to family tradition and undermines parental authority." Another paragraph explains that the chief hallmark of the ultra-conservative is an "absolutist mentality." The term "absolutes"—i.e., "unchanging truths"—has been negatively construed, even though most people believe that there are certain unchanging truths.

Section 11.- KEEPING COOL WITH THE LITMUS TEST

On page 16 of the Washington State's attack manual, "What's Left After the Right?", we learn in a sidebar at the margin about another tactic favored by professional manipulators: " [P]romote what we do rather than react to our critics ...." In reality, this doesn't happen very often, as our adversaries get caught up in emotion the same as we do. Then they go to "attack mode" instead of staying focused on their mission. That's good news for you. You can make use of such lapses, provided you keep a "cool head."

The manual warns ominously that conservative parents tend to run for school board positions as well as local and state political offices; push for the recall and/or defeat of those who do not represent their beliefs; make every attempt to serve on state and local curriculum committees; participate in telephone blitzes and other informational campaigns; lobby for legislation like home schooling bills and "baby Hatch Amendments"; file lawsuits; and volunteer as classroom aides to get inside the classroom. These actions are treated as somehow unethical.

What is an appropriate response to such "charges"?

You should simply say: *"So what? Your side does all the same things – and with a lot more money, too. The ACLU initiates frivolous lawsuits; the NEA subsidizes candidates for school board elections. So, it's a draw. We both work to promote our people and our beliefs. Tell me something I don't know or talk about something else."*

Angry denials ("We do not do that!") are defensive and doomed to fail.

One interesting fact the writer of the **NEA manual** let slip was that some 30 percent of the resistance comes to school programs and policies from SCHOOL STAFF. This says a lot about just how little agreement there is within the profession, despite the NEA's public relations to the contrary. Our side needs to capitalize on that. All teachers, principals, administrators are not happy with the liberal agenda in education.

Even so, the **NEA manual** instructs educators to sell the advantages of the offending curriculum, project, activity or text —to promote it, instead of addressing any of the complainant's concerns: an offensive strategy.

THE 14-POINT STALL

On page 75 of the **NEA manual**, there is a questionnaire entitled "Circumventing Censorship or Your Radical Right IQ." The respondent (usually someone seeking a position of leadership) is supposed to mark "yes," "no," or "don't know" beside each entry. Here is your first taste of "the litmus test."

Among the more interesting survey items are:

- Has your district actively defined and promoted the concept of intellectual freedom for both the staff and community?
- Is there an academic freedom policy or negotiated academic freedom clause in the teachers' contract?

- Would you say, currently, that the vast majority of the teaching staff, administrators, and board of directors agree on a definition of academic freedom?
- Has your district kept track of those community organizations who (sic) are most likely to be influenced by Far Right literature, speakers, tactics and pressure groups?

What can we tell from the four litmus-test questions above?

1. The issue will be framed for the benefit of complainants and the media.
2. The questions will use some variation of the slogan "academic freedom."
3. Resisters are smeared as not-so-bright, irrational censors.
4. The reader of the manual is being flattered.

If you figured all this out already, move to the head of the class.

The next significant (and telling!) suggestion from the manual is for school districts to set up a resource center: a rolling "Far Right Cart"—no kidding!—that "will make…censorship resources available to staff," complete with easy loan/check-out instructions!

Can you imagine what would happen if our side set up a far-Left cart complete with political tips?

Now we move closer to the more thorough litmus test you will encounter should you run for school board or other public office impacting education. Let's look at the scenario which the **NEA manual** sets out on page 110, concerning how to handle an incident of Right-Wing "censorship."

Situation: A primary school library assistant (a school staffer) approaches a teacher, Board member, or Administrator about removing a set of books called Inner City Nursery Rhymes that contain profanity. The Board member looks through them and notices that they do, in fact, contain some profanity, **and is offended as well**. A check with the other elementary school across town reveals that it has the books also. What to do?

Now for the zinger: ". . . **[T]he assistant,"** states the manual, **"belongs to the local Eagle Forum group."**

That's enough right there to determine the strategy. Even though educators themselves may be offended by the books, *the manual advises that they not be removed, since doing so "implies permission for self-censorship to occur any time, by any person."* The advised seven-point response, under "Helpful Tips" (their page 112), is fairly typical of rebuttals by school officials to any complainant, staff-generated or otherwise:

- "Let the complainant know you have heard the concern and that you will assist in every way possible to have the issue addressed ...." (In other words, be polite and pretend you care).
- "Refer [the assistant] to the district's policy and procedure for consideration of controversial materials." (Procedure, otherwise known as "red tape," makes an excellent method for gaining both time and control. It wastes the complainant's time, frustrates and tires him out.)
- "Explain that the concern must be submitted in writing." (How many times have you heard that? More time-wasting—and you'd better be articulate.)

- "Do not suggest that the book be removed ...." (Translation: Don't give in until and unless the fire hits the fan.)
- "Inform the building and central office administration, or whoever in the district has been designated as the one responsible for handling curricular controversy issues." (That is: Pass the buck and prolong the process .)
- "Initiate the process for reconsideration...[b]ecause the book 'appears' ... to be inappropriate, but ALWAYS follow the process." (Translation: Cover your behind. Process over substance tends to solve all problems.)
- "Take time to re-familiarize yourself with the appropriate and related district policies." (Translation: Look for loopholes.)

The above lesson was the NEA's laughable attempt at handling fallacious arguments. What it reveals, however, is our adversaries' seven-point working strategy for addressing complaints from the public (paraphrased below):

1. Be polite and pretend to care.
2. Waste as much of the complainant's time as possible.
3. Maintain the upper hand and the psychological advantage.
4. Don't give in, even if you suspect the complainant is right, because doing so sets a dangerous precedent.
5. Pass the buck and prolong the process.
6. Cover your behind, just in case, and place process over substance.
7. Review and re-review policies for loopholes you can use.

Under another "Helpful Tips" section, it is suggested that complainants be warned that any "free floating accusations will not be tolerated and legal action against them may be a consequence"—a hilarious threat in light of the fact that readers of the NEA manual will have so far endured some 100 pages of free-floating accusations, with no mention of "legal consequences."

Under "Countering Far Right Tactics" (page 121), one finds additional guidelines:

(a) "Challenge the credibility of the attacking group ..."

(b) "Attempt to resolve confusion regarding misstatements, ... clarify ..."

(c) "Avoid giving legitimacy and emphasis to Far Right charges ..."

From these, one can add the following three "translated" versions to the seven points we just assembled:

8. Stereotype and label the opposition;
9. Promote the activity/curriculum and say you're "clarifying the issue"
10. Marginalize the critics.

The ASCD/ECS attack manual suggests additional ploys:

- Invite a group of critics to meet with you, listen attentively, then politely say that you will "take their comments 'under advisement' if common ground cannot be found"; and that your "job is to serve the greater good."
- If any "national experts" are being brought in by the group to talk to community members, find out who is paying for them to come, what interests they represent, and whether

they represent the views of a vocal minority—then treat them accordingly.

- Make it clear to complainants, wherever possible, "that [the] community or state has decided that children should develop" whatever skills and abilities which the activity in question supposedly transmits.

For the sake of brevity, these can be summarized in the following way and added to the list of "stall strategies" above:

11. Pretend to take criticisms seriously by "taking them under advisement."
12. Always claim to be "serving the greater good"—i.e., the collective.
13. Marginalize any experts representing contrary views prior to their appearance.
14. If possible, claim decisions are set by state or other authorities.

Now you have 14 tactics your adversaries will use against you. Memorize them. Whatever arguments a principal, superintendent or teacher may use to rebuff your criticism, by whatever means a facilitator or change agent may "work" your group over, regardless of any fallacies you may be able to identify and counter, the thread that will run through them all can be found in the above 14 points. Your opponent may or may not avoid direct confrontation, may or may not go on the defensive, may or may not commit a fallacy, but if s/he is trained at all, you can count on the 14-point stalling tactic.

CAMPAIGNS AND ELECTIONS

Most attack manuals, including the NEA's, devote several pages to elections and campaigns, especially those related to school boards. In truth, most educators would be just as happy to see school boards go away and all power transferred to federal or state education agencies. But since that is happening only sporadically (so far), considerable attention is devoted to elections and campaigns.

According to the NEA manual, the aim of involvement in school board campaigns is to scuttle attempts by "crazy conservatives" and to deal with "censorship." ***So, no matter how "local" you think an election is, tremendous resources will be poured into the campaigns to ensure a pro-NEA/big-government outcome.*** Indeed, in the second paragraph in the section entitled "Participating in the School Board Election Process," it states: **"Every candidate for school board should be carefully interviewed by the education association and/or a patron committee early in the campaign regarding candidate views in educational issues."**

Notice the manual did not say "interviewed by the community, parents, citizens, or taxpayers." The interview that counts is the one by "the education association" (that's the NEA and/or its state chapter and proxies). "Its patron" means some proxy/puppet organization. The following list of questions serves as the litmus test to weed out conservative candidates.

Fail that, and you're in for a long, dirty haul. These questions are quoted from the NEA manual verbatim below:

- What are your top five objectives if elected to the school board?
- What is your view of the purpose of public education?
- How would you define the concept of academic freedom?
- How much latitude should the individual teacher have in his or her classroom?
- What is your view of the proper role of the school board and its members in relation to selection and retention of instructional materials?
- Do you have any specific changes you want to make in the curriculum offered in our district? If so, what and why?
- How would you respond to a parent who wants the district to limit access to or remove books from the library?
- Who should determine broad educational objectives? Specific course objectives?
- What limits, if any, would you like to see for employees teaching controversial issues?
- Who will you look to for advice on instructional matters?

What are the NEA-preferred responses to these questions? Let's take them one at a time:

- *Do you have any specific changes you want to make in the curriculum offered in our district? If so, what and why?*

The NEA's preferred response will be that you would "like to strengthen academic freedom."

- ○ *How would you respond to a parent who wants the district to limit access to or remove books from the library?*

The NEA-preferred response will reiterate the seven-point process used with the library assistant earlier on, being careful always to fall back on procedure and process. Worded appropriately, your response would go something like this—an abridged version of the 14 "stall tactics" previously listed:

- Be polite and caring.
- Buy time with procedures and paperwork.
- Maintain the upper hand and, therefore, the psychological advantage.
- Don't give in, even if you suspect the complainant is right.
- Consult a designated individual in the central office and prolong the process.
- Cover yourself.
- Place process over action.
- Review and re-review policies for loopholes you can use.

- ○ *"Should sex education be taught in the schools?"*

Anything but an enthusiastic affirmative on this question and your candidacy is dead.

- ○ *"How do you describe your position on separation of church and state?"*

Again, the NEA-preferred response is that religious mention and allusions to religious practice in schools are violations of the Constitution.

- *"Where could the district spend less money? Where could it spend more?"*

Preferred answers will be somewhat locality-dependent, but in general, less emphasis on academic materials and more on school counselors, psychologists, gym equipment, and so on will pass the litmus test.

- *"Do you believe more education dollars should go to early childhood education? Why or why not?"*

A hearty 'yes' is expected, together with copious politically correct verbiage about getting kids 'socialized.'

LONG-TERM ACTION PLANS

All three attack manuals call for long-term action plans to create alliances, or partnerships, between educators and various leftist organizations that promise to "run interference" for the education establishment against the public. The idea is that when trouble arises, there will be a certain familiarity, or loyalty, between the liberal/leftist organization in question and local policymakers to clear the path for a radical agenda. Toward that end, the following activities typically are recommended by our adversaries as part of any long-term strategy:

- "Train a cadre of educators and community representatives to be process facilitators for panels, forums, and discussion groups."

- "Conduct surveys and compile results to determine the 'real' issues that need to be addressed." (The manual's use of quotations marks around the word real implies that statistics will be "cooked" and survey questions slanted.)
- "Develop an Academic Freedom and School-Community Cooperation Philosophy." (Several examples are provided. The idea here is to publicize and distribute the "academic freedom" slogan in an attempt to head off criticism of activities, curriculums, programs, or materials.)
- "Apply for grants to do exemplary projects. Look into... foundation funding. Tell the state department [of education] that with a little help, you'll give them a state wide model that will knock their socks off."
- "Put in a 'Rumor Stopper' hot line where complaints and questions can be immediately addressed."
- "Hire a full-time, high-powered public relations specialist."

The above provides a glimpse into the extent of funding the left is willing to spend molding public opinion. Our candidates, on the other hand, tend to be average moms and pops having little or no financial backing. They simply "feel called upon" to run. Occasionally they win, but their lives are made miserable and most soon throw in the towel. We must put more effort into planning, financing and running candidates, even for small races like school boards. The left wants to preclude the possibility of any charismatic winners on our side.

PROPER QUESTIONS FOR SCHOOL BOARD CANDIDATES

(compliments of EdWatch of Minnesota (1998-2010)

The following are some suggested questions for you to use to help evaluate your school board candidates. Notice that these questions are worded so as to give the prospective candidate just enough rope to hang him/herself, inasmuch as the interviewee can't tell exactly what answer you want!

ACADEMIC QUESTIONS FOR CANDIDATES

1. Do you support a *primary* emphasis on teaching basic skills (e.g., reading, grammar, spelling, arithmetic) or on social and psychological adjustment?
2. Do you support the use of intensive, systematic phonics or do you prefer "whole language" to teach children how to read?
3. Should children be able to read by the end of the first grade?
4. Do you support or reject teaching abstinence as the standard for unmarried teenagers and as the only method with a proven tack record in preventing sexually-transmitted diseases?
5. How do you approach the issue of illegal drugs?
6. Do you believe the topics of homosexuality and alternative lifestyles should be included in classroom discussion?
7. What resources do you use to teach about Sustainable Development in science classes?
8. Do you teach programs that emphasis vocational awareness in elementary school?
9. Do you support academic programs for high-performing students to complement the No Child Left Behind Act's focus on low-performing students?

10. Would you emphasize or de-emphasize world citizenship in civics curricula (i.e., the International Baccalaureate, the GLOBE program, the Center for Civic Education's curriculum)?
11. What do you teach concerning the proper role of government in society, and what resources do you cite for this topic?

POLICY QUESTIONS FOR CANDIDATES

1. What is your opinion on the collection and maintenance of data on student health, performance, attitudes, behavior, and family, as well as academics, in computerized databases?
2. What's your view on mandatory mental-health screening for students?
3. How do you feel about school-based health clinics, and should they be tasked with performing examinations, providing immunizations and medications, and dispensing birth control device and abortion referrals?
4. What is your opinion on accepting outside grants from special interests?
5. What changes in class scheduling would you recommend if you had the chance?

PARENTS' RIGHTS QUESTIONS FOR CANDIDATES

1. What is your view on school districts collecting student data using non-academic student surveys involving students' personal behavior, values, attitudes, beliefs, or those of their family and friends? (e.g., Teen Screen, Minnesota Student Survey, Search Institute, etc.)
2. Do you support requiring parental permission on non-academic student surveys?
3. Do you support the universal pre-school concept?
4. Do you support all-day, year-round kindergartens?
5. What is your view on home-schooling?
6. How far should parental rights regarding the upbringing and education of their children extend, in your view?
7. How far do you think schools should go in promoting good behavior and ensuring student safety on campus: Surveillance cameras? Pat-downs? Metal detectors? All-day campus police presence?

In the end, all politics is about perception. Politics isn't about capability or ideals or merit or track record. Those things all show up after the election is over. It is your task to bring these issues to light ahead of time.

This, then, ends the advanced level of the seminar/workshop on psychological warfare. You may move on to the Final Exam.

SELF-TESTS

NOTE: The MID-TEST (which covers the General-Intermediate Course) and a Special Exam on Education Issues are located below, as this is the end of the entire course of study. Answer keys to these self-tests follow.

MID-TEST

MULTIPLE CHOICE: Select the best answer for each question, as indicated.

1. Why do citizens with traditional values always lose when they try to reason with representatives of the education establishment?

a) Because they are not exhibiting team spirit.
b) Because they generally don't understand the principles of rhetoric (argument).
c) Because they don't know that teachers and administrators have been "prepped" ahead of time to expect "nutty" parents to assail them and/or school policies.
d) Because they mistakenly believe that teachers and other members of the Education Establishment are truly interested in being their partners.
e) Because most lay citizens don't think like marketing agents.
f) All of the above.

2. What is the primary reason why those holding to traditional values typically lose when they serve on task forces, curriculum committees, and focus groups?

a) Because lay citizens tend to be shy about speaking their mind.

b) Because parents and average citizens are overly impressed by educators' credentials.

c) Because parents and lay citizens never gain the psychological advantage.

d) Because lay citizens don't understand consensus-building strategies.

e) Because educators don't listen to parents' legitimate concerns.

3. The most important key to controlling any controversial discussion is:

a) To bide your time; wait for an opportune moment to inject comments.

b) To deprive the opposition of any chance to control the debate, or agenda.

c) To know who is funding the opposition.

d) To ensure that lots of people from your side participate in the discussion.

e) To arrive armed with plenty of documentation that proves your position.

f) To be continually deceptive and evasive in your comments.

4. The allusion by ancient Chinese texts on battle regarding the need "to drive the enemy's leaders insane" means that:

a) Blatant hypocrisy can work in your favor.

b) You can frustrate people enough that some will "go over the edge."

c) It is possible to create a crisis environment where nothing is logical.

d) You can cause your enemy to squander his resources by lashing out aimlessly in all directions.

e) All of the above.

f) Two of the above.

5. The long-term purpose of generating a phony consensus on an issue is:

a) To prove to lawmakers that the consensus is what the community wants.

b) To get group members mad at each other so they can't solve anything.

c) To create an "irreconcilable conflict."

d) To confuse the issue.

e) To promote certain viewpoints over others.

6. A vicious cycle of resentment, reaction, and government response is helpful to radical groups primarily because:

a) It creates chaos.

b) It causes "thought disruption."

c) It permits government to impose Byzantine regulations and red tape.

d) It allows more crimes to be federalized.

e) It pits political activists against each other.

7. In tailoring radical causes for the media (print or electronic), the most important consideration *to your opponent* is:

a) Getting out the facts—at least their version of the facts.

b) The psychological impact of the promotional materials.

c) Maintaining credibility in the eyes of the public.

d) Regrouping and recouping their losses.

8. Particularly in matters of education, what factor has put our side at the greatest disadvantage?

a) We care how many people get hurt and our opposition doesn't.

b) Our opposition has bought up more media outlets than we have.

c) Our opposition can afford to go on the offensive and we can't.

d) Our adversaries view teenage abortion, suicide, and drug addiction as social problems instead of as sins or crimes.

e) The police can no longer protect our children.

9. The short-term purpose of psychological manipulation and PR is:

a) To legitimize, then institutionalize, unpopular and bogus policies quickly.

b) To change the meanings of words we thought we were understood.

c) To embarrass and confound conservatives.

d) To ensure a bitter confrontation between opposing factions.

10. When a radical initiative gets a "black eye" (a bad reputation), policymakers may do any or all of the following, except one:

a) Change the name of the program.

b) Restructure or repackage the program and try later.

c) Mandate the program.

d) Dump the program.

e) Replace the program with another one that is similar.

11. Effective marketing depends upon all of the following except one:

a) Catchy slogans.

b) Gross or captivating images.

c) Factual accuracy.

d) Appeals to accomplishment, intelligence, or fear.

e) Targeting a demographic and socioeconomic market.

12. The hardest-hitting psychological manipulation techniques were devised or piloted by all except one of the following (mark one answer):

a) Kurt Lewin

b) The Tavistock Institute and Clinic

c) Theodor Adorno

d) The Institute for Social Research

e) Teachers' unions

13. Select the three most basic axioms our counterculture adversaries use to set up a psychological environment:

a) Redefining.

b) Setting up irreconcilable conflicts.

c) Isolating your opposition.

d) Labeling opponents.

e) Repetition of key phrases and slogans.

14. In a group setting (meeting, committee, task force, etc.), you, as a knowledgeable activist, must do which TWO of the following in order to have a real voice in the discussion (i.e., to avoid being "Delphi'ed")?

a) Frame the debate.

b) Have a visible network of friends with you.

c) Bolster the confidence of weaker group members.

d) Bring a lot of information about the proposal or program with you.

e) Distribute methods of taking on a facilitator at the meeting.

15. A teacher promoting a particular worldview in the classroom may tell parents s/he is doing any or all of the following, except which one?

a. Indoctrinating pupils.

b. Engaging in academic freedom.

c. Pursuing his right to free expression.

d. Transmitting important societal values.

16. Successful brainwashing or indoctrination is possible only if one has:

a) Framed the debate.

b) Disrupted the subjects' thought processes.

c) Rooted out a subject's emotional support system.

d) Terrorized the subject.

e) Discredited the subject.

17. In the vernacular of professional manipulators, a *vacuum* is:

a) A lack of any preconceived opinion on a topic.

b) A disrupted thought pattern (lapse) which renders the subject vulnerable.

c) That place in the psyche that once contained a belief system.

d) Feelings of alienation and isolation.

18. To heighten a person's suggestibility, it is necessary to:

a) Provide a steady diet of conflicting and confusing images and words.

b) Disrupt the subject's thought process.

c) Weaken the subject's emotional support system (parents, priest, rabbi).

d) All of the above.

19. A teacher is described by behaviorists in terms of all the following, except:

a) A clinician

b) A facilitator of learning

c) An instructor

d) A mentor

e) A learning practitioner

20. Educational indoctrination works primarily because:

a) Students have to memorize the materials.

b) Students won't get a Certificate of Mastery (diploma) unless they pass tests indicating they accept the new ideas.

c) Parents aren't paying attention to the lessons kids get.

d) Biased lessons bypass the conscious mind and shoot directly for the gut.

e) The federal government is unlawfully involved in curriculum decisions.

21. The "escape route" and "road to safety" referred to in the Principles of Psych-War are best described as:

a) Bait.

b) A captive setting.

c) A reprieve.

d) A solution.

22. According to behaviorist-progressive educators, the primary role of the teacher is to:

a) Tell children outright what to think.

b) Teach character (values).

c) Serve as an adjunct to parents.

d) Covertly influence opinions.

e) Transmit knowledge.

23. One Psych-War principle is "bringing one's opponent to the field of battle." To accomplish this, an adversary might:

a) Do a negative review of a book written by the opposition in a popular publication so that people would get a bad impression of it.

b) Boldly confront us whenever we hold meetings.

c) Writing letters to the editor in the city's most widely read newspaper blasting our views and candidates for office.

d) Invite a few of us to a public meeting.

e) Turning us away when we try to attend one of their meetings.

24. According to Sun Tzu's Principles of Psych-War, what does it mean to "lure your enemy to the north and strike in the south"?

a) To lull the adversary into a false sense of security.

b) Bait, then switch tactics.

c) Ignore your opponent so that he doesn't get a forum from which to speak.

d) Have representatives of your side in as many places as possible.

e) Keep profiles on as many of your opposition's members as possible.

25. The Republican Party is currently in disarray, with factions arguing about key issues. Turf battles have surfaced among conservative organizations, all competing for funding and/or legitimacy in the media. Which Rule of Psych-War does this situation represent the most?

a) The rank-and-file are angry and have lost confidence in their leaders.

b) Numbers alone are conferring little advantage in the political arena.

c) The opposition has wearied its opponents by keeping them constantly occupied.

d) Accomplishment has been demanded of people who have no talent.

e) An escape route has been provided and everyone has fled.

26. Why would a facilitator insert an irrelevant, but hot-button comment into an argument?

a) To draw out and label opponents.

b) To bring attention to a point the group may have missed.

c) To divert attention from the subject of the argument.

d) To generate more discussion among group members.

e) To subtly insert the facilitator's own opinion into the discussion.

27. Why is the sentence "This program creates a level playing field" considered a good marketing ploy?

a) Because it appeals to expertise.

b) Because it appeals to popularity.

c) Because it functions as a distraction.

d) Because it creates a false analogy.

e) Because it appeals to most people's innate sense of fairness.

28. If someone calls you a "fundamentalist Christian" in the course of a group discussion, you should do what? (Select 2)

a) Strongly deny it even if it's true.
b) Avoid denials even if it's not true.
c) Explain to everyone where the term "fundamentalist" comes from.
d) Treat it as a distraction and remind the group of the topic.
e) Discredit the person who said it.

29. The three keys to countering a psychological environment once already established by a facilitator are (Mark 3):

a) Take the "floor" and redirect the discussion.
b) Determine the real issue.
c) Locate the people who agree with you and launch a verbal counterattack.
d) Don't give the facilitator anything to work with until you have a good idea why you are really there.
e) Establish your thesis and don't let it go.

30. A facilitator/agitator's "trump card" or "operating rationale" is that:

a) Most people never agree on anything anyway.
b) Most people are irrational and have no firm opinions.
c) Most people have never heard of a "facilitator."
d) Most people tend to agree with educators.
e) Most people like to think they are rational and can work things out.

31. Which of the following would be LEAST likely to send a facilitator to a community to generate a consensus for a program, project or policy?

a) The Republican or Democratic Party.
b) A nongovernmental organization (NGO).
c) A trust or endowment.
d) A foundation or think-tank.
e) One of the U.S. Department of Education's regional research Labs and Centers.

32. Our opposition's attack strategies include all of the following except...

a) The snoop survey.
b) Sowing seeds (planting ideas) that de-legitimize our concerns.
c) Rebutting our research or public testimonies point by point in writing.
d) Preparing and distributing how-to/beware manuals.
e) Having the teachers' union screen all school board candidates.

33. The purpose of making sure a complainant goes through a series of proper channels to "process" his or her complaint is to:

a) Get all the concerns "on the record" and "out in the open."

b) De-legitimize the complainant.

c) Avoid misunderstandings and mistakes.

d) Wear down the complainant with delays and red tape.

e) Force the complainant to retract his objection.

34. If a program, activity or policy comes under attack after it is implemented, the opposition's strategy may include any one of the following except (select two):

a) Going on the defensive and take on the detractors.

b) Going on the offensive and vigorously promote and the program.

c) Doing away with the program.

d) Making the program "voluntary."

e) Reviewing policies for loopholes in order to retain the program.

35. School board candidates can expect any number of questions to come up in their campaign. All of the following are sure bets, except which one?

a) Do you have any specific changes you want to make in the curriculum offered in our district?

b) How would you respond to a parent who wants the district to limit access to or remove books from the school library?

c) Who should determine broad educational objectives?

d) What limits, if any, would you like to see for employees teaching controversial issues?

e) Which method of teaching reading should be stressed in our district over the next five years?

True-False:

_____ 1. It is easier to manipulate the thought processes of a single individual than it is to manipulate the thought processes of a group.

_____ 2. Morale and psychological factors are often more important than sheer numbers in winning a war.

_____ 3. Deception and surprise are two key principles of battle.

_____ 4. Never "blowing your cool" in a controversy means always being polite and giving the other fellow the benefit of the doubt.

_____ 5. The allusion by ancient Chinese texts on battle regarding the need "to drive the enemy's leaders insane" can be taken literally.

_____ 6. A psychologically controlled environment makes it easier for the provocateur to frame the debate.

_____ 7. The typical leftist or liberal is careful to study everything our side writes or says so that we are forced to defend our views at every turn.

_____ 8. Political liberals of the 1930s and 40s are the same as today's counterculture adults.

_____ 9. Abe Lincoln's adage about not being able to fool all the people all the time is still correct.

_____10. People are usually aware of their own belief systems.

_____11. There is no point in counting on having any base of support in task forces and other meetings or forums.

_____12. Control of the psychological environment produces a springboard to indoctrination or brainwashing.

_____13. Control of the psychological environment determines what topics people discuss and think about and for how long.

_____14. The Science of Coercion refers to security police who monitor school hallways.

_____15. The purpose of always giving your enemy an escape route is to give him an alternative to losing a battle and save face.

_____16. Slogans help to redefine terms.

_____17. If people hear the same phrases and slogans often enough, they will come to question their validity.

_____18. The purpose of an "academic freedom" clause or policy is to ensure that real academics are taught.

_____19. "Clarifying the issue" means to promote the activity in question.

_____20. To gain support of the Education Establishment, a school board candidate should heed the advice of the community on matters of instruction.

Short Answer: Fill in the blanks with the best response or answer the question.

1. It is harmful to an activist movement if its leaders are confused because

2. Why do ease of parole for violent criminals, politicized and arbitrary child-endangerment laws, and failure to monitor serious offenses like burglary while fixating on minor offenses like parking and speeding together help create a vicious cycle of resentment and reaction, while generating a disrespect for legitimate authority?

3. Name the four key components of all psychological manipulation.

4. What is the difference between a *dictionary* definition and a *working* definition?

5. What is the difference between *indoctrination* and *brainwashing*?

6. Name four of the five basic steps to indoctrination?

7. All warfare is based on ________________.

8. One of the most critical aspects of Psych-War, at least for the underdog, is the ability of a highly intelligent individual to be able to appear to be stupid; to be strong, but appear dull strong; to be vigorous and energetic, but appear fatigued, and so on. This is not for everybody, but for those who can do it, why is such capability important?

9. How is it possible to isolate people who are already in a group?

10. How is it that our adversaries can demonize the practice of labeling and stereotyping, yet do it consistently themselves to prejudice the public?

11. How does one keep control of the psychological environment?

12. Every hypothesis (or theory) is based on ________________.

13. Appeals work because they are based on ________________

14. In what ways does a facilitator who is under attack try to pass the buck and get parents or the community off his/her back?

15. What does it mean to be told that your criticisms have been taken "under advisement"?

ESSAY (non-graded):

How should the following situation have been handled?

A newspaper editorial described how groups of disenfranchised citizens were brought together to "discuss" what they felt needed to be changed at the local level. A written compilation of these "discussions" influenced the writing of the city/county charter.

What happened is that the facilitator began by appearing neutral, lulling everyone into a false sense of ownership about the discussion. She worked the crowd to establish a good-guy/bad-guy role. Anyone disagreeing with the preferred viewpoint ended up appearing as the bad guy, the others as rational and "with it." This had the effect of sending a clear message to the rest of the task force: Unless they wanted the same treatment, they best keep quiet. Once the opposition had been identified and alienated, the facilitator again became the good guy (friend) again, and the agenda and direction pursued a predictable course.

Next, attendees were broken up into smaller groups of seven or eight. Each had its own facilitator—taken, of course, from "selected" participants. The group facilitators then proceeded to steer their charges to pre-selected issues; no other topics were entertained.. Participants were encouraged to put their ideas and even disagreements on paper, with the results to be compiled "at a later time," ostensibly to assess "what the community wanted."

When asked later about how the various responses were compiled, most participants believed that the facilitators took all the concerns and presented both the pros and cons to superiors. When asked: "How do you know that what you wrote down was incorporated into the final outcome?" The typical answer was: "Well, I wondered about that, because what I wrote didn't seem to be reflected in the final draft. I guess my views were in the minority."

Unsurprisingly, the outcome turned out ***not*** to be reflective of the community's views.

MID-TEST ANSWERS

MULTIPLE CHOICE:

1. f
2. d
3. b
4. e
5. a
6. c
7. b
8. a
9. a
10. d
11. c
12. e
13. d
14. a
15. a
16. c
17. c
18. d
19. c
20. d.
21. a
22. d
23. d
24. b
25. a
26. c
27. e
28. b, d
29. b, d, e
30. e
31. a
32. c
33. d
34. a
35. e

TRUE-FALSE

1. F
2. T
3. T
4. F

5. T	11. F	17. F
6. T	12. T.	18. F
7. F	13. T	19. T
8. F	14. F	20.F
9. T	15. T	
10. F	16. T	

SHORT ANSWER:

1. Because it helps to destroy morale.

2. Because the discrepancies eventually serve to confound and confuse people and make them perpetually angry—"drive them crazy."

3. Redefining, re-directing, marketing, and consensus-building.

4. The dictionary definition is the one we commonly understand and refer to; the working definition is the experts' redefinition, usually expanded version, of a term.

5. Indoctrination is more sophisticated in that its purpose is not merely to redirect or disrupt the thought process, but to systematically root out a person's emotional support system.

6. Sweep away the emotional support base; disrupt rational thought with series of confusing images; insert desired ideas into the vacuum; condition the subject; test, survey and, if necessary "recycle" the subject.

7. Deception.

8. Because you can inject the element of surprise and throw off the facilitator.

9. Using peer pressure; pitting one faction against the other; escalating tensions to draw out the people you want isolated; alienating and ostracizing those with non-preferred views.

10. Through repetition and slogans.

11. Frame the debate.

12. Assumptions or "givens."

13. The power of suggestion.

14. Send the complainant to the state education agency or cite the federal government.

15. That your viewpoints will be ignored.

Non-graded Essay Question: The scenario will generate varied answers, but the bottom line is that the facilitator should have questioned up front concerning his or her affiliation, who paid for his or her services and other queries that would prompt this person to reveal the "preferred" pre-determined outcome. In other words, get the facilitator to reveal his/her agenda before you are goaded into revealing yours.

SPECIAL EXAM ON EDUCATION ISSUES

The following questions (answers follow at end) are used as fodder for talk show hosts as well as for legislators and activists.

QUESTIONS:

1. Why are school tests (including those from previous years) held tighter than the Pentagon Papers (i.e., exempted from the Freedom of Information Act) so that parents are refused access even after-the-fact?

2. What is it called when school tests and surveys ask children what magazines are in their homes, whether parents have a dishwasher, and the family's favorite vacation spots?

3. What is "predictive computer technology," and how is it useful to experts in determining a student's future employability?

4. What is the primary focus of college course work for prospective educators, including curriculum and testing specialists?

5. Describe a process called "thought disruption" and explain how it affects learning.

6. What is "cognitive dissonance," and how does it compromise parent-school cooperation?

7. How have terms like "remedial" and "disability" been redefined so that parents erroneously believe their child will get special help?

8. How “individualized” is an IEP (Individual Education Plan), and what rights do parents have once they sign it?

9. What legal loophole permits the federal government to become involved in state and local curriculum?

10. What is a psychological “marker” (used in behavioral screening instruments), and why is “strong religious belief” considered a marker for mental illness?

11. What level of privacy does the term “confidential” confer?

12. What federal law prevents Information Brokers from combing secure databases for “value and lifestyle” information and cross-matching it with political criteria or other public and private records?

13. What is “data-laundering”?

14. What is the scope of school-related computer cross-matching?

15. How are the principles of advertising used by educators, and what are the two primary axioms of advertising?

16. How could schools really assure nondiscriminatory testing and placement?

17. What is the most important ethic that today’s teachers are expected to transmit?

18. What new law institutionalizes mandatory psychological evaluations in schools; what is the umbrella legislation it falls under, and what was the name of the pilot program?

19. What are the long-term effects of psychiatric drugs on growing bodies?

20. What do education experts consider the primary purpose of education?

ANSWERS to SPECIAL EXAM ON EDUCATION ISSUES:

1. The rationale is that the validity of all tests and surveys will be compromised if a layperson sees any of them.

2. Psychographics: "the study of social class based on the demographics of income, race, religion and personality traits."

3. By combining responses pupils provide via self-reports and situation-based questionnaires with psychographic data, statisticians can predict how a child will likely react to events in future years. This capability can be turned into a political litmus test by college and job recruiters.

4. Behavioral psychology.

5. "Thought disruption," a technique launched in 1940s Germany, means interrupting the train of thought so that logic cannot proceed. The continual interruptions built into the school day impede a child's ability to concentrate.

6. "Cognitive dissonance" means an unresolvable conflict resulting from attempts to reconcile two opposing "truths" simultaneously. When educators discredit parental teachings, youngsters cannot choose between two opposing "authorities."

7. These are buzz-terms for warehousing kids deemed "uneducable" by the system. Teacher training deals with emotions, not learning methods.

8. Signing an IEP gives the school control over future education-related decisions and provides virtually no individualized help.

9. "Compelling state interest."

10. Markers are "risk factors." Firm religious belief has been linked to the dogmatic, authoritarian, and delusional personality.

11. Confidential means "need to know," not "anonymous." Data, including a person's identity, are shared with "approved" entities.

12. No federal law yet prevents database searches and cross-matches. Legal experts can't seem to craft a law that differentiates between legitimate and illegitimate cross-matching.

13. "Data-laundering" means deleting or changing existing data surreptitiously to circumvent #12, above.

14. The SPEEDE/ExPRESS is the largest school collection-and-transfer "engine." WORKLINK, developed by the Educational Testing Service, provides a link to employers.

15. Advertisers were the first to employ psychographics as a means of targeting a market. The primary axioms are: (1) "All

consumer behavior is predictable," and (2) "Consumer behavior can be changed." The key is finding what makes the target population tick. School "tests" and surveys, rife with opinion-oriented questions, provide this key. Curriculum becomes the advertising package for social change.

16. Class placement, curriculum, and teacher training built around learning processes (spatial reasoning, perceptual speed, auditory memory, etc.) is nondiscriminatory.

17. "Interdependence": The group is more important than the individual and consensus more important than principle.

18. The New Freedom Initiative (via the President's New Freedom Commission on Mental Health); the enabling legislative vehicles are the No Child Left Behind Act through incentives under the Individuals With Disabilities Education Act (IDEA) and State Incentive Transformation Grants (SIGs); and the pilot was the Texas Medication Algorithm Project (TMAP) under then Governor George W. Bush.

19. Psychiatric drugs haven't been around long enough to know.

20. "To change the students' fixed beliefs." - Dr. Benjamin Bloom

GRADING SCALE:

19-20 correct = Fit for public office

17-18 correct = Study up for debates

14-16 correct = Easily manipulated by special interests

12-13 correct = Frankly, my dear, you don't know diddly about schools.

SPECIAL APPENDIX ON ENVIRONMENTAL ISSUES

--with special thanks to Michael Shaw (Freedom Advocates) and Michael Coffman (Environmental Perspectives)--

Because environmental issues have assumed so much importance over the past five years, not only in education, but as a tool to restructuring the entire U.S. economy, foreign policy, and imposition of a socialist redistribution of wealth, it is essential to discuss what Sustainable Development really means in order to comprehend how it is being used to indoctrinate young Americans and slant the news for adults. The goal is to have Americans so internalize the tenets of SD, which is routed in an initiative called Agenda 21[2] that its premises become non-negotiable and the public sees its socialistic goals as necessary and property, including the watering-down and eventual elimination of property rights, United Nations involvement in both American judicial and foreign decisions and the psychologizing of U.S. education at the expense of substantive learning.

Michael Shaw of Freedom Advocates (among others in footnote #2) describes SD as a tool of global corporatists, both on the Left and Right, as well as anarchist libertarians and communist anarchists (who are, by the way, by no means defunct). As Vladimir Lenin directed, "few comrades need understand new world objectives and philosophies, most are

2 Log onto Freedom Advocates at www.freedomadvates.org; to Environmental Perspectives at www.epi-us.com; and to the American Policy Center at www.americanpolicy.org/sledgehammer-action-alerts/.

simply useful idiots' who help us achieve our objectives." That truism still holds.

Shaw shows that SD is global fascist-Communism. "The Democrat and Republican parties play contrived roles in furthering world governance under the guise of implementing Sustainable Development 'policy'. At its root, sustainable policy seeks: the abolishment of private property; the adoption of a [United Nations approach to] "social justice"; an economy based on public-private partnerships ... in order to eliminate free enterprise, and [a] dramatic reduction in the number of human beings. The role of designated and financed sustainability leaders, including political leaders, is to destroy the political will of a once free people who [so far] wish to remain free.

Sustainable Development uses the environment as an excuse to cover its real purposes. Those purposes are the establishment of a transformed system of American Justice and Economics—which, of course, will vastly alter our constitutional liberties.

The intent is for these new systems to produce a new ideal, in Hegelian fashion, to produce a "brand new" synthesis of two opposing concepts that will be packaged to appeal to the unschooled (or mis-educated) masses (see the **General Introduction** to the **Beginner-Intermediate** section of this manual): i.e., a consensus. The "authorities" behind these new systems primarily advocate for a vastly empowered United Nations. Many of these useful idiots are power-seekers right here in the U.S. who do not believe that average citizens are competent to run their own lives, much less their own country. Thus, do they labor to establish a one-world governing body—a "benevolent dictatorship" (with themselves hopefully sitting at the Board of Directors) alternately doling out "grants" and withdrawing "human rights," as best serves the interests of this obscenely wealthy, elite caste, for lack of a better term, that presumably has the "best" interests of their underlings at heart. The fact that "benevolent dictatorships" invariably turn malevolent somehow escapes them.

To ensure that these new ideals and the ensuing policy directives are accepted, they target in particular the schools and the sciences, which, due to 40 years of watered-down curriculum, they can be reasonably assure d that most people will not understand to begin with, and will not be motivated to study because of (a) all the bureaucratic regulations imposed upon citizens that waste their time and exhaust their energies, and (b) prurient entertainment options that also waste time and exhaust the emotions.

SPECIAL APPENDIX ON SOCIAL STUDIES

Anything out of the United Nations is not going to be about American-style justice before the law or rewarding human ingenuity. It will be a Marxist rehash touting *equality of outcomes*. The Universal Declaration of Human Rights (UDHR) parallels the Convention on the Rights of the Child (CRC) in its seeming guarantees concerning freedom of thought, conscience religion, opinion and expression. Just scanning, it all sounds like our own Constitution and Bill of Rights.

Except they aren't.

Article 29 gives the game away when it warns that the "rights and freedoms" iterated there "may in no case be exercised contrary to the purposes and principles of the United Nations." So, who's in charge if the U.S. signs on? The United Nations or the United States? Undoubtedly, the United Nations.

To that end, social studies and its UNESCO[3] educational component that advertises its wares as the International Baccalaureate (IB) bares no resemblance to the Baccalaureate of the 1950s, which at least emphasized basic subjects for young grade-school-aged children along with rigorous, substantive tests. Today, the emphasis is rooted in The Earth Charter, which comprises the backbone of IB science, ethics, literature and history programs, because that is UNESCO's approach to foreign

3 United Nations Educational, Scientific and Cultural Organization

policy issues. As I wrote in June 2010[4], the primary elements of the Earth Charter are:

- World federalism.
- Earth worship (pantheism).
- Socialized medicine.
- Income redistribution among nations and within nations.
- Eradication of genetically modified (GMO) crops.
- Contraception and "reproductive health" rights (inc., legal abortion).
- World-wide "education for sustainability"—i.e., planned communities in which populations are told where they shall live.
- Debt forgiveness and different standards for third-world nations.
- Adoption of gay rights and the right of children to all sexual materials and literature.
- Elimination of any right to bear arms.
- Environmental extremist positions, including global warming, bans on pesticides and genetically enhanced vegetables.
- Setting aside biosphere reserves where no human presence is allowed, which means the government may come in and take your land for its own higher purposes — something that is now being debated in a case before the U.S. Supreme Court.

4 The New American, June 2010.

The Declaration of Independence and the U.S. Constitution are fundamentally opposite from the U.N.'s Universal Declaration of Human Rights. A few examples:

- The right to bear arms — UDHR has no right to bear arms.
- No double jeopardy — UDHR does not prohibit double jeopardy.
- Church/state separation — UDHR promotes earth-worship spirituality.
- Limited government — UDHR has no limits on government.
- Reserved powers — UDHR has no reserved powers.
- Recognition of natural law — UDHR does not recognize natural law.
- Guarantee that property cannot be taken by government without just compensation — UDHR has no such guarantee.

If one doesn't look too closely, UDHR appears to mimic the American creed—that is, the principles of the Declaration of Independence and the U.S. Constitution: that all men and women are created equal; inalienable rights of life, liberty and the pursuit of happiness, that government exists to protect those rights, and limited government. But the IB program, promotes the U.N. position of guaranteed "happiness," not just its pursuit, as indicated earlier in this manual. It also lacks the references to universal truths and values that once were staples of the American classroom. International curriculum standards promote UDHR as being an evolution of previous principles.

Social justice is another construct of the Left and is not to be confused with traditional American justice. It is not the *action-based* model (i.e., equality before the law) familiar to Americans prior to 1970, but rather an equity-based model (i.e., parity and equality of outcomes) rooted in socialism. The various covenants, declarations, proclamations and protocols iterated in the U.N. documents are humanistic constructs, versus religiously based standards. Only the banner of "human rights" serves to provide a cloak of legitimacy.

"Justice" in the U.S. was initially grounded in "action." *Acts*— what you do to me and what I do to you — are perpetrated by either individuals or groups, and deemed legal or illegal according to specified laws. In the 1960s, "justice" in America started being nudged away from this definition by the U.N. and its supporters and moved toward "fairness"—i.e., ameliorating social *conditions*, which is an entirely different enterprise.

As the Founders saw it, the largest problem with past political systems was that all were predicated on the idea that human beings are foolish and reactive. It was thought that unless people were watched, regimented and scared half to death, a country would self-destruct, taking its elites and leaders down with it. So, the individual was consigned to insignificance. Common wisdom had it that all should go toward the good of the monarch (the State or ruling elite), which in turn provided some measure of security for the groveling masses.

The Framers decided to reverse this logic and did something unprecedented. They geared governance to the *best* in human nature instead of to the worst. Somehow, the Founders figured out that when governments construct policy so that it is geared negatively—i.e., toward the worst, most irresponsible persons, under the mistaken assumption that doing so will rein in bad conduct—all they get back is more irresponsibility. So, why not try rewarding honesty, decency and hard work—the best in human nature? In so doing, they produced the highest standard of living on earth.

Moreover, "social justice" is reactionary and represents a regression. Yet, the packaging is modern, and 40 years of untaught or misrepresented constitutional documents have made the sale easier to swallow by those under 45, particularly those who have had no personal exposure to real life under other governments.

So, today's much-ballyhooed IB is committed ***not*** to a melting-pot concept, but to globalism and multiculturalism. Accurate history, correct geography, honoring perspectives or even other nationalities all wind up in a hodge-podge called "diversity" or "multiculturalism," which is more lip-service than substance. Like SD, IB upholds the collective, not the individual; world government is celebrated over national sovereignty; centralization of power is honored over local control. That is why "social studies" are mostly about minimizing Western culture.

This is also the essence of SD, Agenda 21 and why they are suddenly selling in the marketplace of ideas. It is not selling so well, of course, among rural landowners whose livelihoods are farming, ranching and producing energy. They are working hard, walking uphill through a glue of bureaucracy and privilege generated in Washington.

About the author...

Beverly Eakman is an Educator, 9 years: 1968-1974, 1979-1981. Specialties: English and Literature.

Science Editor, Technical Writer, and Editor-in-Chief of the official newspaper of the National Aeronautics and Space Administration's Johnson Space Center, 1976-1979. The technical piece entitled "David, the Bubble Baby" was picked up by the popular press and turned into a movie starring John Travolta.

Chief speech writer, National Council for Better Education, 1984-1986; for the late Chief Justice Warren E. Burger, Commission on the Bicentennial of the US Constitution, 1986-1987; for the Voice of America Director, 1987-1989; and for U.S. Department of Justice, Gerald R. Regier, Director of the Bureau of Justice Assistance, 1991-1993.

Beverly Eakman is the author of six books that include education, data-trafficking, tracking and monitoring, privacy, mental health issues, and political strategy.

Website: BeverlyE.com
To schedule media interviews
E-Mail: bkeakman@gmail.com

Also by B. K. Eakman

A Common Sense Platform for the 21st Century
Midnight Whistler Publishers

Cloning of the American Mind: Eradicating Morality Through Education,
Huntington House Publishers

Educating for the New World Order

Microchipped: How the Education Establishment Took Us Beyond Big Brother
Halcyon House Publishers

WALKING TARGETS: How Our Psychologized Classrooms are Producing a Nation of Sitting Ducks
Midnight Whistler Publishers
http://www.midnightwhistler.com

The above books can be ordered through Amazon, at Barnes & Noble online bookstores, as well as by special order at most specialty bookstores.